INTIMACY WITH JESUS

AN INTRODUCTION

Richard J. Huelsman, S.J.

PAULIST PRESS
New York/Ramsey

Cover: Emil Antonucci
Illustrations: Marili Hellmund

Acknowledgments: Excerpt from *Revelation of Divine Love—Juliana of Norwich* translated by M.L. del Mastro. Copyright © 1977 by M.L. del Mastro. Reprinted by permission of Doubleday & Company, Inc. • Excerpt from the English translation of *The Roman Missal* © 1973, International Committee on English in the Liturgy, Inc. All rights reserved. • Adaptation of material from *The Jesus Prayer* by George A. Maloney, S.J. Reprinted by permission of Dove Publications, Pecos, New Mexico. • Excerpt from *Pray* by Richard Huelsman, S.J. Copyright © 1976 by The Missionary Society of St. Paul the Apostle in the State of New York. Used by permission of Paulist Press. • Excerpt from Thomas Merton, *Collected Poems of Thomas Merton.* Copyright © 1947 by New Directions Publishing Corporation. Reprinted by permission of New Directions. • Excerpt from p. 10 in *The Mind of Jesus* by William Barclay. Copyright © 1960, 1961 by SCM Press Ltd. Reprinted by permission of Harper & Row, Publishers, Inc. • Excerpt from *Who Is Jesus of Nazareth?* by John P. Kealy, CSSp, Dimension Books, 1977, Denville, N.J. Used by permission. • Excerpt from article by Rev. John B. Healey. Used by permission of the *Brooklyn Tablet.* • Excerpt from "Affectivity and Sexuality" by William A. Barry, S.J., *Studies in the Spirituality of the Jesuits,* Vol. 10, Nos. 2 & 3 (March-May, 1978, pp. 92-94). Used by permission of The American Assistancy Seminar on Jesuit Spirituality. • Excerpt from *The Natural Health Bulletin,* edited by Carlson Wade, © 1974, Prentice-Hall, Inc. Published by Prentice-Hall, Inc., Englewood Cliffs, New Jersey 07632. • "I Dream" by Langston Hughes, from *American Negro Poetry.* Copyright © 1945 by Langston Hughes. Reprinted by permission of Harold Ober Associates Incorporated. • Quotation from *How to Read and Pray the Gospels, copyright* © 1978, Liguori Publications, One Liguori Drive, Liguori, Missouri 63057. Used by permission. All rights reserved. • Material adapted from "A Method of Praying the Gospels!" by Francis Buck, S.J., *Review for Religious,* (May-June, 1981, p. 404). Used by permission of the publisher. • Quotation from "The Last Things," by Gerald O'Mahony, S.J., *The Way,* Vol. 21 (January 1981), the Jesuit quarterly *Review of Spirituality,* London, England. Used by permission. • Excerpt from *Bread for the World* by Arthur Simon. Copyright © 1975 by Paulist Fathers, Inc. and Wm. B. Eerdmans Publishing Co. Used by permission of Paulist Press.

Imprimi Potest:
Michael J. Lavelle, S.J.
Office of the Provincial
Detroit Province, Society of Jesus
January 19, 1982

Imprimatur:
Edward J. Herrmann
Bishop of Columbus

January 4, 1982

The Imprimatur and Imprimi Potest are official declarations that a book or pamphlet is free of doctrinal or moral error. No implication is contained therein that those who have granted the Imprimatur or Imprimi Potest agree with the contents, opinions or statements expressed.

Library of Congress
Catalog Card Number: 82-60587

ISBN: 0-8091-2492-0

Published by Paulist Press,
545 Island Road, Ramsey, N.J. 07446

Printed and bound in the United States of America

CONTENTS

CHAPTER ONE
THE FIRST STEPS
TOWARD INTIMACY WITH JESUS

CHAPTER TWO
COMMUNICATING IN PRAYER

MEDITATIONS

APPENDIX

CHAPTER THREE
GROWING IN PRAYER

INTRODUCTION

MEDITATIONS

APPENDIX

INTIMACY WITH JESUS

Jesus,
I'm so glad
you are here.
It makes me
realize
how beautiful
my world is.
          —*Author Unknown*

Do you think that times are bad, or
that life is coming unglued, or
that nothing seems to have meaning?

Are you somehow looking for *more* from
life, as well as to be doing something
to improve the way things are?

Then this book, the first of a trilogy,
is for you. It is about the love and
following of Jesus, and should repay you
richly for effort expended.

But before getting into its contents,
a word of gratitude to Rosanne Stalter, Sr. Mary
Jane Masterson, Joan and William Redding,
and Rev. Michael Becker for innumerable
kindly helps and suggestions; to Rev. James
Smith, Sr. Marie Shields and the people of
St. Christopher's parish, whose warm
companionship and reactions to piloting
were such help in shaping the work,
to my typist Barbara Anderson,
and finally to my sister, Sr. Rose Huelsman, IHM,
for being the sister she is to me.

Every effort has been made to secure permissions
to reprint copyrighted material. If any has
been inadvertently omitted, notice would
be appreciated.

INTRODUCTION

This is a very personal book. Feel free to mark it up, take notes, use it as you will. The predecessor to this book, *PRAY*, is a course in how to pray and follow Jesus. This book is a course in how to pray better, and follow more *intimately*. It is for those who have already met Jesus and want only to follow in love. It is also for those who, seeing Jesus walking along the road, have just barely gotten the courage to ask "Where do you live?" "Come and see," He says. So they turn to follow; though not entirely without wondering whether they should have asked, or what they might be getting into!

Intimacy with Jesus, as well as *PRAY*, owes much to the *Spiritual Exercises* of St. Ignatius, especially Week I, and "The Kingdom" in Week II.

Intimacy with Jesus goes on some assumptions:

that many yearnings of the human heart are meant to be deeply satisfied in Christ, yearnings for meaning in life, for a high sense of self-worth, for love and fulfillment, for security and joy, and for a sense one is growing to be One's Best;

that deepened friendship with Him is possible even for the ordinary person precisely because He is the one inviting it. And what He invites He will enable to happen;

that following Him involves kindness and thoughtfulness to people near at hand, especially at home and work; as well as concern for the larger human condition such as the Bomb, polluted air, economic injustice and systems seemingly out of control;

that on some days what one needs from a spiritual life more than anything else is just help to survive. "Lord help me make it through another day." Maybe you know the feeling;

that finally, when all is said and done, you are searching for God. Hungering for God would not be putting it too strongly. If you are, *Intimacy with Jesus* is for you.

Intimacy with Jesus is to help you walk closer to Jesus. It invites you to share with Him so much that is human. The book has ten chapters, with ten meditations each. For fullest impact use the meditations in sequence.

Each meditation begins with introductory comments. The Meditation proper is followed by several Seed Thoughts. These seed thoughts are optional. Sometimes you may need them to start you thinking; at other times you may choose not to use them unless you take more than one day on a particular meditation. They are drawn from the saints, spiritual writers, the author's prayerful reflections and those of the people who piloted the course.

It is recommended that you go through the book slowly, especially over meaning-filled material. Depth of insight and relish for the material are more important than the amount of material covered. *Far* more important. One idea can change your life. Linger where you find profit.

Group Use

Intimacy with Jesus is for do-it-yourself use or for group use. For group use, participants could share insights over one or more meditations already made, or let a member preview a few meditations and select one for prayer or discussion. For prayer you might try to listen together for what the Lord could be saying. For discussion you might try to relate the meditation to human situations in the family, at work, school, or recreation, or discuss whether and how it speaks to our times.

Meeting frequency? If concerned mostly with learning to pray, and with questions, directions and problems, one meeting every two weeks over a chapter works well. When discussing content, weekly meetings over half a chapter are useful, and often just one meditation will be enough for discussion. The course, however, is flexible.

Sometimes just one or two meetings can be enough to launch people into prayer on their own, all the more if a leader/director is available for private conference.

Intimacy with Jesus would be fine fare for Advent, Lent, or personal retreat. It could well be a follow-up to Genesis II, Romans VIII, Christ Renews the Parish, or any of the other currently available programs for prayer or renewal. Charismatics would find it helpful for between-meeting prayer. Families could pray over one meditation at a time. It is highly adaptable; the possibilities are endless.

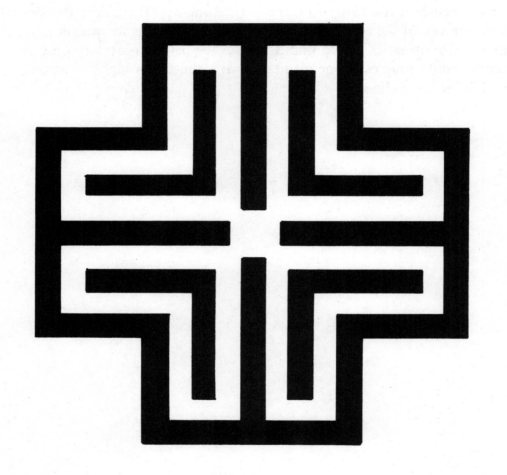

CHAPTER ONE

**THE FIRST STEPS
TOWARD INTIMACY WITH JESUS**

INTRODUCTION

HOW TO MEDITATE

After reading the meditation and Scripture passage slowly, *slowly*, grow *quiet* for a while and *listen*!

While quiet, let the thoughts of Scripture and the meditation resonate and roam about in your heart and soul. Just sort of "stay" with them. Be watching or waiting for some inner reaction or response to occur, some thought or feeling, or practical application. "Lord what are you saying to me?"

Use that thought or feeling-reaction to converse with the Lord. Use your own words. Talk from your own heart in any way that seems to want to come, including expressing doubts or fears, as well as love or thanks.

If no reaction occurs, read the Scripture again, this time vocally, more slowly and thoughtfully. Be alert for what attracts or repels you as you read, and pray over it right then and there. Perhaps a word or phrase will strike home. If it does, repeat it several times. Then converse, praise, ponder, question, ask for, relish, or argue over the insight in your heart in any way you feel moved. Do so for *as long as* you feel moved before reading further.

Even just to sit in a kind of wordless silence while you are wondering, gazing, or relishing God, the scene, Jesus, or the insight—this is good prayer too.

In short, read; listen; then converse with the Lord as you feel moved. If it seems appropriate, make a resolution as to how to live out the meditation during the day. For example, as to how it might affect your relating to other people.

If You Are New to Meditating

Some of you will find meditating a new experience. It is a form of prayer that offers some content, something of the Christian message that is important or profound. It also leaves you free to ruminate, pray, converse with the Lord or interact as you will. So, *Intimacy with Jesus* provides content material (basically Jesus' message), and much freedom to respond.

Don't expect lights to flash. Do expect gradually a deeper and deeper sense that you are getting close to God and that you are really engaged in very personal interaction with Him. You may start to feel this rather quickly or only after a few weeks. If you don't seem to sense at least some contact with God after a month of effort, consult someone learned in prayer or a "spiritual director."

This book is written so as *not* to do all the work for you. It is written only to prompt your response to the Spirit, to help start the wheels rolling over content of importance. The real "event" comes when you talk, and listen to what God may want to say through insights, feelings, and impulses to act or to rest in His presence.

A nice length for this kind of prayer is twenty minutes, give or take a few. If new at prayer or if your life is pressured, this may be too long. In that case, start with just three or four minutes faithfully every day. Assign a regular time and place to Be Sure It's Done. At that time, read the text and scripture passage slowly and thoughtfully. Then continue to mull over the materials during the day. It's often best to pick just *one* thought from the content, whatever moves you *most*, and mull over that.

Gradually, over the months and years, you will find your own style of praying. Different temperaments and body types can respond quite differently to the same text. You yourself may *re*-make a meditation and find it talks to you quite differently than the first time. It can be a delightful experience to discern *your* way. Do try, grow, experiment, and seek the Lord in now this way, now that, noting what best brings you in contact.

3

When all else fails, follow the rules! Go back over the basics as spelled out occasionally in these meditations.

But don't get rule-bound. *It's really very simple.* Read the text. Then say to the Lord: "Lord, what are you saying to me?" Then grow quiet and listen! And to broaden your prayer, sometimes ask: What are you saying to us all?

If You've Been Meditating for a While

If you have been into prayer for a while, you may want to move beyond discursive or conversation-type prayer. When you feel a distaste to meditate (in the sense of reasoning and thinking about a topic), you may be being called by the Lord simply to let the material engage your *emotions* or affections immediately upon reading. If so, just stay with that feeling-response, praise, thanks, wonder, awe, fear, doubt, peace, joy, remorse, sorrow, whatever . . . .

So, your approach might be to *read* the material and then—by-passing all conversation—rest in the feeling it stirs. You hardly converse with the Lord at all. You simply contemplatively gaze at the total scene or at the Lord, and you reach to God with whatever affection or emotion occurs.

Thus in the First Meditation of this chapter, "Feeling Good About Myself," you might want to enjoy a quiet feeling of thankfulness and security as you rest in God's unconditional love, and your prayer might be largely resting in that experience.

MEDITATION

1

FEELING GOOD ABOUT MYSELF

In almost everything they do, people like to know: "Am I looking good? Am I doing OK?" Often they feel they are not; so they become Down on themselves and wonder if they are worth anything. It then seems hard to love *anyone*, even Jesus.

This experience is so common that it is worth noting: Ultimately your self-esteem does *not* depend on achievement or how you look in the eyes of other people. You are of incalculable worth just because you exist. Why? Because you are a person whom the Father created out of special fondness for just you! And you are a redeemed sister or brother of Jesus who died for you as personally as if none other existed. You are also a tablet on which the Spirit would like to write a message for the world, a lute or guitar on which God would like to play a love song. And that holds true regardless of your past or present sins or failings. How fortunate can you be?

MEDITATION

"Jesus, tell me, why am I entitled to feel good about myself?"

Read Isaiah 49:15-16.* Then talk with the Lord about how greatly He loves you and about your unconditional value in His eyes. He will *never* stop loving you.

Let Him tell you about your good points and best qualities and about your possibilities for growth. Let Him affirm you. He would like to. Why not let Him?

*(Isaiah)
Can a mother forget her infant, be without tenderness for the child of her womb? Even should she forget, I will never forget you. See, upon the palms of my hands I have written your name . . . .

SEEDS

The above sounds so good, do you really believe it?

Try to relax into enjoying one great sensation: feeling good about you. For God's sake and your neighbor's, you owe it to yourself.

It is not what you are, and not what you have been that God considers, but what you wish to be.

Walk tall, daughter or son of God. You are born to royalty.

Can you do anything today to help others feel OK about themselves? "Could I be sensitive today to someone who is 'Down'?"

It's all right to admit to yourself that you feel Down, if you do. Feelings are feelings; and if they are there, they are there. But it might be well to consider how these, like any source of disease, can best be managed. Negative feelings are not helpful to growth—or love.

(God speaking)
"You
special, miraculous, fragile,
fearful, tender, lost,
sparkling ruby,
emerald jewel,
rainbow-splendor person,
it's up to you.
Would it embarrass you very much
if I were to tell you
that I love you?"
    —*Author Unknown*

You shall love your neighbor *as* yourself.
    —*Jesus*

Reflect that these words could be just as truly addressed to every person in the world, every single one. What does this say to you?

MEDITATION

2

I AM IMPORTANT TO JESUS

Besides being able to feel good about myself because Jesus loves me, what am I to make of my present attraction to him? Indeed, why am I feeling *any* attraction unless it is He who notices me, and He who by His Spirit is reaching out, drawing, and touching me?

MEDITATION

"Jesus is noticing me!"

Read John 1:35-39* slowly and thoughtfully. Hear in this passage Jesus' call to yourself to become a person who will walk with Him as follower and friend. Perhaps not as an apostle but possibly as a disciple. Converse with the Lord about this freely given invitation to walk closer, more intimately with the most wonderful Person who ever walked the earth. "Lord what are you saying to me?"

You may be utterly frank in your conversation, in the same way the people of Palestine were when they talked with Jesus. He would like that. If you are bursting with thanks, say so. If diffident, or wondering whether to accept, say so.

*(John)
Jesus turned. "What are you looking for?"
"Rabbi," they said, "where do you live?"
"Come and see," he replied.

SEEDS

"Jesus, when in years past has it seemed that you were reaching out to me? How might you be doing so now?"

God has created me
to do Him some definite service.
He has committed some work to me
which He has not committed to another.

I have my mission.
I may never know what it is in this life.
But I shall be told in the next.

I am a link in a chain,
a bond of connection between persons.
He has not created me for nothing.
I shall do good. I shall do His work.

He may take away my friends,
He may throw me among strangers.
He may make me feel desolate,
make my spirits sink,
Hide my future from me—
Still, He knows what He is about.
              —*John Henry Cardinal Newman*

Without me, there would be a hole in the universe!

Your spiritual life *is* one long awakening to how God is revealing himself, inviting, touching you personally. Have you noticed?

Do you really, deep down believe you are important to Jesus?

Could you help anyone else believe in their worth in his eyes?

How about the other persons in my life, the ones I care about, do business with, find irritating—are they called to intimacy with Jesus too?

MEDITATION

3

EVEN THOUGH I'M IMPERFECT, JESUS LOVES ME

"How can Jesus love me? I'm full of faults, and don't pray very much." Such thoughts or feelings of guilt or unworthiness can be obstacles to Jesus' desire for intimacy. The sooner we let Him love us as we are, the better.

He wants to love us, warts and all, just as He loved Mary Magdalene, Peter, and every faulty sinful human being He ever came in contact with. There is mystery here: God loves us even in sin; and even *when* sinning! Just as a mother may not always approve of what her child is doing, yet doesn't she love her or him just the same?

MEDITATION

Jesus really loves me, even though . . . .
This may be hard to believe, but . . . .

Read John 8:1-11* and then reflect as moved. Read the texts slowly and thoughtfully. This is a meditation to rejoice over Christ's forgiveness of yourself, and to be glad of your possibilities for growth, no matter how bad the past . . . or the present. And remember, when God forgives, He forgets.

11

*(John—Woman Taken in Adultery)
"*Woman, where did they all disappear to? Has no one condemned you?*" "*No one, sir,*" *she answered. Jesus said: "Nor do I . . . . "*

SEEDS

Ordinary human life is pretty much rising and falling; trying many times, failing again and being endlessly forgiven. But that is the way life is. He knows that! His glory is in being the Forgiving One. Our glory is in a glad and joyful accepting of His pardon.

"Faith is the courage to accept acceptance."
— *Paul Tillich*

"Thank you! Thank you because . . . in spite of all my sins I am loved and forgiven!"

> Love bade me welcome; yet my soul drew back
> guilty of dust and sin.
> But quick-ey'd Love, observing me grow slack
> from my first entrance in,
> Drew nearer to me, sweetly questioning
> if I lacked anything.
> "A guest," I answer'd, "worthy to be here";
> Love said, "You shall be he."
> "I, the unkind, ungrateful? Ah, my dear,
> I cannot look on Thee."
> Love took my hand, and smiling did reply,
> "Who made the eyes but I?"

"Truth, Lord; but I have marr'd them; let my shame
Go where it doth deserve."
"And know you not," says Love, "who bore the
    blame?"
"My dear, then I will serve."
"You must sit down," says Love, "and taste My
    meat."
So I did sit and eat.
    —*George Herbert*

It belongeth to the proper
goodness of our Lord God
courteously to excuse man.
    —*Juliana of Norwich*

It helps other sinners feel loved and
forgiven by God if they are loved and forgiven
by us. May they reciprocate!

It seems that Jesus had a special love for the not-so-perfect, the
sinners, the crippled, the lame, the outcasts, the unloved. Am I
in any way like these people?

MEDITATION

4

IS MY RESPONSE WHOLEHEARTED?

Sometimes people put off trying to deepen their relationship with Jesus. Deep down, they would like such a relationship but they fear it might involve time or sacrifice. Love does ask such things.

Or maybe they have tried love before and failed.
Or they are too bitter to pray.
Or they are overly attached to what displeases the Lord.
Or they are "too busy."
Or they acquired a bad parent image that they transferred to God.
Or they just can't get started.
Or they can hardly believe how loving and
      caring Jesus really is for them.
Or for yourself personally, what *is* in the way?

Note: If you have even the smallest desire to deepen a relationship, these meditations can help. And if a quiet glow is already there, ask Jesus to bring it to flame. Be assured. With a little effort on your part, He will. The best things in life are still free. Enjoying the love of Jesus is one of these. And in Jesus' mind it's for you.

MEDITATION

"Jesus, is anything holding me back from you?"
Unbind me from fear, reluctance or a sluggish
heart!"

Read Luke 10:27*; and Romans 8:35-39*. Notice Jesus' call for whole-hearted love and Paul's joyous response. (Ask for these!)

> *(Luke)
> *You shall love God with all your mind, all your heart,*
> *all . . . .*
> *(Romans)
> *Who shall separate us from the love of Christ? Trial*
> *or distress, or persecution or hunger . . . ?*

SEEDS

"Call me louder, Lord. Or open my ears."

> Lord, take my heart, for I cannot give it to You;
> Lord, keep my heart, for I cannot keep it for You.
> —*St. Augustine*

> Batter my heart three personned God; for you
> As yet but knock, breathe, shine and seek to mend;
> That I may rise and stand, o'erthrow me and bend
> Your force to break, blow, burn and make me new.

> I like an usurped town, to another due,
> Labour to admit you, but Oh, to no end;
> Reason, your viceroy in me, me should defend,
> But is captured and proves weak or untrue.

Dearly I love you and would be loved fain,
But I am betrothed to your enemy:
Divorce* me, untie or break that knot again
Take me to you, imprison me, for I,
Except you enthrall me, never shall be free,
Nor ever chaste except you ravish me.
       —*John Donne*

*Free me from your enemy

"Why, why oh Lord do I feel attracted by you? I
suppose it sounds strange to ask, but why?"

I wonder if Jesus ever wonders why strong and instant
response to His love isn't universal and overwhelming.
"Is it something in the contemporary air . . . ?"
Was it always thus?
What is keeping so many away?
Is it due to anything I am doing, or not doing?

Praying for others who are wrestling with the Lord
can be very helpful, to them and to yourself.

MEDITATION

5

HOW CAN I SENSE JESUS' LOVE?

Since Jesus is inviting you closer, what would this mean for everyday life? If you wanted to sense more intensely how much He is loving you, what would you do right now to open yourself more?

MEDITATION

"How shall I open myself more to your love? Let me count the ways . . . . "

For this meditation talk with the Lord about such matters. If nothing comes to mind, simply read the questions above again, then remain in wordless quiet before Him for a few moments, waiting for any interior movement with "upraised hands." Expectant, quiet waiting is good prayer. If nothing comes, try reading the following Seeds.

SEEDS

You might simply want to open your eyes, ears and senses to God's goodness in the sights, sounds and delights of being alive. On all sides are the works of His love. God made us so

He could love us. And we love Him so well by letting Him! Are you breathing? Then He is holding you in existence because He loves you. Are you seeing? Then He is holding up the whole world for you to scream in delight at his goodness.

Or you might want to cultivate a close-to-conscious joy that Jesus has given Himself to you in friendship with no strings. You walk about feeling glad!

You might think of God our Father as a Worker for us his children, holding up the universe and decorating everything with beauty. In gratitude you might want to offer your work as a prayer, saying before each principal task: "This is for you." And afterwards, "Hope you liked it!" Or, "We thank you for counting us worthy to stand in your presence and serve you."

One might want to think of how Jesus is loving us through friends. And through a variety of workers he is providing for our needs. Through physicians he is healing illnesses. Through the Church he is fighting evil. Through ordinary Christians he is working to make society more humanly sensitive. And he is doing all this *for me*.

You might opt for a running conversation with Him all during the day, as with an indwelling and very, very real companion.

When eating alone you might think of Jesus sitting on the other chair, and proceed to share a meal, thanking Him for it, and for the gift of taste to enjoy it.

Or how do you suppose some saint, or the first disciples, or a friend might find God in the midst of everyday life? People who are predominantly more active, or more thoughtful, or more emotional, may find quite different ways. Experiment!

One of the keys to many of these practices is the Heart. One doesn't always "think" of Jesus during the day. One just does whatever she or he is supposed to be doing—with gladness because somehow it is for Him; and He is near. It is a union of mood or emotion. This avoids trying to "think of two things at once," one's work and the Lord.

MEDITATION

6

THE "JESUS PRAYER"

The Jesus Prayer is the practice of reciting "Lord Jesus, have mercy on me a sinner" in rhythm with one's breathing. Some other short prayer may be used similarly. The text below is adapted from *The Jesus Prayer* by George A. Maloney, S.J.

The use of this prayer began in the early centuries after Christ, when thousands of men and women went to the desert to escape sin-laden surroundings and enter into more interior prayer. They would accustom themselves to remain close to God with the constantly repeated "Lord Jesus Christ, Son of God, have mercy on me a sinner."

In such a simple prayer the early Christians experienced Jesus as both Lord (the first half of the prayer), and Healer (the second half). As they breathed IN, they associated that action with reverence and love for Jesus as Son of God. As they breathed OUT they cried in humility, Have mercy and heal.

Some prefer two complete breaths: "Lord Jesus/Son of God//have mercy/on me a sinner." With practice, this prayer can become so much a part of life that the prayer goes on almost as a reflex even in busy occupations. Then the Lord seems always near.

MEDITATION

Try the Jesus Prayer:

As a prayer experiment, try this practice during daily living. Use "Jesus, Son of God, have mercy on me," or "Jesus," or "My God, my God," or any other short prayer that suits you.

Try letting it run through your head and heart like a "song you can't get out of your mind" during the day whenever you think of it. While driving or while doing chores might be times to try this gentle prayer that gives a sense of Jesus' closeness.

It is helpful to synchronize with breathing, though feel free to find *your* way to use it.

SEEDS

This method works beautifully for deepening a childlike trusting sense of God as Father. Thus, "Abba, Father, I belong to you." Try this some morning or evening instead of meditation.

When using this mantra (short prayer) for a few or several minutes at a time, it will be normal for your mind to wander. As often as it does, just gently bring it back to the rhythmic recitation. Don't strain. Just gently bring your mind back to sensing and enjoying being with God. It is an interesting prayer form.

Try saying the Jesus Prayer in the plural for the needs of the world, or for some group of people. Since Jesus came to show mercy and heal, include those especially who are poor or the victims of injustice.

"Mercy" is well translated "gracious and loving kindness," rather than simply as "overlooking sin." Thus, "Lord Jesus, show me (us) your kindness."

MEDITATION

7

ETERNAL LIFE

Besides the blessings that come in *this* life, what do we who seek and follow the Lord look forward to, in the *next*?

Scripture suggests:

Colossians 3:4	We shall appear with Him
Luke 22:27-30	in Glory, eating and drink-
	ing at His table and judging the
John 17:24	Twelve Tribes; in the com-
John 15:15	pany of Jesus glorified and
I Peter 1:4-7	as His friends; having for
and	our own an imperishable
I Peter 5:4	inheritance which will not
	fade; and which will include
I Corinthians 15:41-42	pride, honor and glory for our-
I John 15:42-44	selves; with bodies transformed
I Corinthians 13:12	and wonderfully glorified.
Revelation 21:1-3	And we shall see God as He is,
I Corinthians 3:8	face to face,
I Corinthians 15:41-42	in a home grand and glorious
Ephesians 6:6-8	where we shall all be rewarded,
Matthew 5:19	but differently, befitting
Matthew 6:19-20	our efforts . . . .
Matthew 10:42	
Matthew 16:27	
I Corinthians 2:9*	So—indeed—"Eye has not seen . . . . "
	But I *so* want to be there!

MEDITATION

What good things will come from loving Jesus?
"Jesus, what have you in mind for your friends?"

Read through the above portrait and give free reign to filling out and personalizing the picture in your imagination. Savor, enjoy, linger as desired. Praise God, allow yourself to be utterly happy! Or look up one or two of the texts and imagine John or Paul as saying them directly to you. Linger over your reaction.

> *(1 Corinthians 2:9)
> *Eye has not seen, ear has not heard, nor has it so much as dawned on man what God has prepared for those who love him.*

SEEDS

What are the blessings in the here and now that come with seeking to love and follow Jesus? What would life be like without Him?

Each action done lovingly in this world increases your capacity to love God and others more intensely for eternity. Loving deeds last forever!

"Eternal Life" is the Opium of the People that lulls them into inaction against evils and oppression, says Karl Marx. This is obviously not what Christianity is about. On the other hand: "Thanks be to God for a little opium as one licks one's battle wounds. And thanks for telling us, Lord, that there is some place where there'll be No More Problems. Some days all I want from life is No More Problems."

24

"Jesus, will my friends be there, and will there be Variety?"
"Yes. And it will be an Endless Spring."

I wonder what Jesus' risen life is like right now, and what my own life will be like with him in the world to come. Whatever I do to cultivate his friendship will surely be counted for gladness on That Day.

> Then I saw
> a new earth
> a holy city
> no more death
> nor mourning
> nor crying
> nor pain.
> —*Revelation 21:1-4*

One of the joys of living for Jesus should be having and feeling love and support from His followers in everyday life.

What might be the ways our society would need to change in order to reflect the glory of the Eternal Kingdom now?

MEDITATION

8

HOW TO MEDITATE BETTER

The invitation to pray is always a gift from God; and the following will encourage intimacy in prayer:

1) A Nice Setting

A set time and "sacred" place for being with God is needed, at least on some days. Time given solely and exclusively to God, when possible in a quiet place. High-Priority time, when you can be reasonably alert and serious, able to enjoy and really enter into what you do. You need not pray EVERY day in this way (though it is a good idea), but at least on some days, even if only briefly. And five or six times a week is recommended.

2) A Warm and Attentive Greeting

Place yourself in God's presence. Sense that He is near, and interested in what you are about to do. Begin with a "sacred gesture": kneeling, standing, lifting your hands, or bowing if you like. To continue, any posture that helps you is suitable. Offer this time to Him as a mark of love; then ask growth in friendship and light about living for Him here and now.

3) Friendly Discourse; Sharing Feelings; Listening as well as Speaking

After slowly reading the meditation and the Scripture passage (reading aloud is helpful), grow quiet for a while. Let its thoughts resonate or roam about in your heart and soul. Wait for some response to occur—some thought or feeling or way to apply the meditation. If nothing occurs, ask "What are you saying?" or "How do you want to touch or love me?" If nothing still comes after waiting a while, read the material again, more slowly and thoughtfully; or use the Seed material to prompt a reaction. Be alert for whatever attracts or repels you and pray over that, right then and there. Repeat phrases that seem meaningful.

4) Finding Meaning

You could also consider how this passage applies to yourself, to your daily life, or to some world problem—or to us all, or to certain persons or groups: Let the Spirit lead!

5) Taking Leave, even with a Certain Reluctance

Have a short heart-to-heart talk with the Lord about what this meditation has meant for you, or about anything that strikes you as you feel moved at the moment. ALWAYS conclude meditating with some such brief, more-intimate contact. Sometimes this might be by a gentle, wordless remaining in His presence.

MEDITATION

How might I meditate better? "Jesus, tell me, what were some of your ways at prayer?"

SEEDS

What is the most moving reason you can think of for giving time to meditative prayer? An important question! (*For several hints, see Appendix A for this chapter.*)

If you have been into prayer for a while, you may want to pray a little differently from the above. (*A suggestion is given at the beginning of this chapter.*)

If repeated meditating doesn't seem to affect your life, try to emphasize a more definite resolution!

Quick meditation: Read and Run; think about it during the day. Quick is better than none, but . . . try not to make the Quick the Usual! (*See also Appendix B for this chapter.*)

For this course, don't be a "compulsive" Seed reader or user. You needn't pray over them all, or *any* at all unless it is helpful.

Again, personalizing this book with notes and reflections can make it a treasure for the future.

To extend your prayer: As you meet people today, try to be conscious of Jesus' attitudes towards people, or towards the daily news.

MEDITATION

9

DOES FOLLOWING JESUS BRING HARDSHIP?

"But won't I have to suffer more if I get more involved with Jesus? Won't I have to give up so much I hold dear . . . fun or pleasure, ambitions, material things, romance, drugs, or drinking? Or won't I feel burdened with religion or less free . . . ?"

Well . . . consider the following:

Jesus came to bring His followers a deep sort of happiness; the joy, peace, and sense of meaning that come with growing toward Him. "Blessed," He said, over and over, meaning "Happy." Sometimes effort, love, and a little trust may be needed. Still, happiness, He said, would result.

From the other direction, a life of sin or totally living for self can seem to promise so much—only to turn disappointing or self-destructive. Of course God will forgive any sin or any amount of selfishness, but we still have to live with the consequences . . . . and can a life-style of *not* following Jesus be that much better?

And, finally, doesn't there come a time in life when, regardless of risk or uncertainty, one realizes that there has appeared on the human scene a Person, such a Remarkable Person, so worthy of utter devotion, that no other choice is as reasonable as to place one's life in His hands? Thomas Merton says it this way:

MEDITATION

(Do you fear loss or hardship in following Him? Pray over the following:)

> My Lord God,
> I have no idea where I am going.
> I do not see the road ahead of me.
> I cannot know for certain where it will end.
> Nor do I really know myself,
> and the fact that I think that I am following you will
> does not mean that I am actually doing so.
> But I believe that the desire to please you
> does in fact please you.
> And I hope that I have that desire in all that I am
>   doing.
> I hope that I will never do anything apart from that
>   desire.
> I know that if I do this
> You will lead me by the right road
> though I may know nothing about it.
> Therefore I will trust you always though I may seem
> to be lost and in the shadow of death.
> I do not fear, for you are ever with me
> And you will never leave me to face my perils alone.
> —*Thomas Merton*

SEEDS

Matthew 8:23-27: "Where is your courage? How little
faith you have!" Then he stood up and took the winds
and sea to task. Complete calm ensued. The men

were dumbfounded. "What sort of man is this," they said, "that even the winds and the sea obey him?"

"Lord, I wonder if I can do it, open myself to You I mean. It would surely be great! But I am so hesitant! Lord, it is You who will have to help me to try. I pray you, help me to try . . . ."

Some lingering reluctance to put yourself and your life completely in Jesus' hands is natural, even after you have done so, or tried to. Talk these feelings over with the Lord, and if they persist, with someone learned and experienced in the ways of prayer.

Mutual support by relatives and friends as well as by the Lord is unspeakably helpful. If one cannot turn to Christian friends when trouble strikes, "to whom shall we go?" Sure, some will likely impose on the generosity of others. They always have and always will. But is that enough reason to close one's heart to those in need? We may suppose that Jesus had the same problem.

Happiness is . . . working through life's problems with Jesus. And in a strange and wonderful way that happens even when taking on the burden of suffering humanity as well as one's personal anguish.

MEDITATION

10

JESUS CARES ABOUT ME

This meditation is an invitation to "let go" of all obstacles or hindrances in relating to Jesus, simply to allow yourself to accept His unconditional love for you personally. Even if feelings like unworthiness hang on, just let them be. Quietly coexist with them as you try to respond in love anyway. Otherwise, they could cheat you of a great benefit.

MEDITATION

"Jesus, how am I special to you?"

Pray over Matthew 16, 18*. Jesus changes Simon's name to Rock. If He changed your name right now, what might it be? Have you a special skill you could use for Him that suggests a name, or does your unique personality offer a clue? (See Revelation 2:17*.) You might reminisce over these matters with the Lord as if sitting with Him in or out of doors, perhaps at a table for two. Let Him tell you how really special you personally are to Him.

> *(Matthew)
> *"I for my part declare to you, you are 'Rock' . . . ."*

> *(Revelation)
> *"To the victor I will give . . . a white stone on which is inscribed a new name to be known only by him who receives it."*

SEEDS

Reflect with Jesus over the history of your friendship during various life-stages. And how do you hope your relationship might grow during the years ahead? Ask Him that it may.

Close friends often have special names for each other. For a while you might repeat lovingly some favorite title or name for Jesus just for the joy of it, in rhythm to your breathing if you like. Then let yourself hear Him repeating lovingly your own name over and over. This may seem very intimate. It is.

It's not always easy to care individually and personally about each person we meet, as Jesus does for us. Should we try? The question is asked because such effort could become more of an effort and emotionally exhausting than one bargained for.

And what about those we will never meet—does Jesus' personal love for me invite me to be actively concerned for those I don't even know?

APPENDIX A

WHY MEDITATE?

Because everyone needs time for silence and reflection. . . .

Because "With desolation is all the world made desolate because there is none who thinketh in his heart" (Isaiah).

Because how better to get deeply impressed with our Father's love, and with Jesus' message, and with your own wonderfulness, and life's unimaginable beauty?

Because how else will we come to love God with a passion?

Because how better to express or respond to the unique relationship which is mine with God?

Because how else to see deeply beneath the surface into the beauty, dignity and worth of persons all about me?

Because there are some things one can do only when alone with the Lord, as when two lovers talk about what is nearest and dearest to them. That is meditative prayer, lovers sharing their hearts and concerns. At times they may just want to sit and look into each other's eyes. That's OK too.

Because meditative praying has unique advantages not offered as fully by Liturgy, Eastern or Centering prayer, rosaries, informal or spontaneous prayer, group prayer, etc. The advantage is content plus opportunity to reflect at leisure. Jesus offers revelation; and He would have us ponder it. For this, meditation is and has been the choice of Christians for generations. It offers the content of Jesus' message plus freedom to respond as moved by the Spirit.

Because every time I meditate God is more glorified, the world is a little better because I prayed, and I will be a little closer to God forever. Not bad!

Because when I meditate I feel better and act better. Not bad either. Sometimes even one's health improves!

And finally, in the face of confusion because world issues add to personal stress, how better to find time to sort things out, get in touch with Jesus' compassion and gather strength to go on!

THREE USEFUL MNEMONICS

1) Four ways to pray, stemming from the Four Purposes of prayer: **ACTS**
   A —*Adoration*—praise, reverence, wonder, awe.
   C —*Contrition*—sorrow, regret, remorse, desire to amend.
   T —*Thanksgiving*—for past or present; for benefits or crosses; in the name of "the other nine," who forgot to give thanks.
   S —*Supplication*—petition for favors or needs, for ourselves, for the world.

2) Three ways to "fly to God," starting from the printed page: Go **TWA**
   T —*Think* what this means. Which idea stands out or appeals most?
   W—*Will* and emotions. How do you feel about it?
       Which feeling comes through most strongly?
   A —*Action*. What is to be done? What most immediately?

3) Ask Basic Questions:
   who
   what
   why
   where
   when
   how
   for whom, and
   does it make any difference?
   For example, who are the persons present in this Gospel scene? Does it make any difference? What is the significant about the fact that they are present?

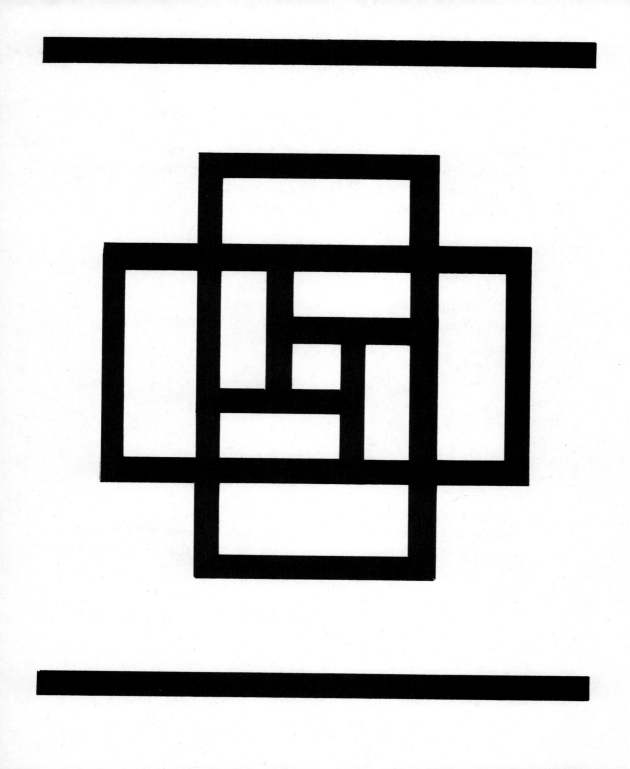

CHAPTER TWO

COMMUNICATING IN PRAYER

INTRODUCTION

DEEPENING A RELATIONSHIP

To get closer to Jesus means not only getting rid of, or deciding to ignore, false guilt and other obstacles (Chapter 1), but getting free to communicate openly and sensitively over all kinds of things . . . as in this chapter.

Prayer Instruction

This is a prayer instruction about how to talk with God simply, directly in your own words, and about anything at all. The idea is to imagine you are in the presence of God and He is speaking to you.

"You do not have to be clever to please me; all you have to do is to want to love me. Just speak to me as you would to anyone of whom you are very fond."

> Are there any people you want to pray for? Say their names to me and ask of me as much as you like. I am generous, and know all their needs, but I want you to show your love for them and me by trusting me to do what I know is best.
>
> Tell me about the poor, the sick, and the sinners, and if you have lost the friendship or affection of anyone, tell me about that too.
>
> Is there anything you want for your soul? If you like, you can write out a long list of all your needs, and come and read it to me. Tell me of the things you feel guilty about. I will forgive you if you will accept it.

Just tell me about your pride, your touchiness, self-centeredness, meanness, and laziness. I still love you in spite of these. Do not be ashamed; there are many saints in heaven who had the same faults as you; they prayed to me, and little by little their faults were corrected.

Do not hesitate to ask me for blessings for the body and mind; for health, memory, success. I can give everything and I always do give everything needed to make souls holier for those who want it.

What is it that you want today? Tell me, for I long to do you good. What are your plans? Tell me about them. Is there anyone you want to please? What do you want to do for them?

And don't you want to do anything for me? Don't you want to do a little good to the souls of your friends who perhaps have forgotten me? Tell me about your failures, and I will show you the cause of them. What are your worries? Who has caused you pain? Tell me all about it and add that you will forgive, and be kind to him or her and I will bless you.

Are you afraid of anything? Have you any tormenting, unreasonable fears? Trust yourself to me. I am here. I see everything. I will not leave you.

Have you no joys to tell me about? Why do you not share your happiness with me? Tell me what has happened since yesterday to cheer and comfort you. Whatever it was, however big, however small, I prepared it. Show me your gratitude and thank me.

Are temptations bearing heavily upon you? Yielding
to temptations always disturbs the peace of your soul.
Ask me, and I will help you overcome them.

Well, go along now. Get on with your work or play or
other interest. Try to be quieter, humbler, more
submissive, kinder, and come back soon and bring me
a more devoted heart. Tomorrow I shall have more
blessings.
　　　—Author Unknown

Try to learn to pray from your heart!

Comment: And we might add, are you disturbed by the immensity of the
problems facing our country and our world: economic problems,
unemployment, the plight of the poor, racial exclusion, persecution
and the denial of basic human freedoms? You can bring these concerns
also to the Lord.

MEDITATION

1

PHYSICAL APPEARANCE

"Jesus slept on the beach last night!"
"What did He look like?"

One of the great gaps in our knowledge of Jesus is
that we do not know what he looked like. In regard to
this tradition was divided. One line stems from
Isaiah's picture of the Suffering Servant. "His
appearance was so marred, beyond human semblance"
(Isaiah 52:14). "He had no form, no comeliness that
we should look at Him, and no beauty that we should
desire Him" (Isaiah 53:2). Arguing from this, Irenaeus
said that Jesus was weak, inglorious, and without
grace. Origen said he was small, ill-favored, and
insignificant. Cyril of Alexandria even went to the
length of saying that He was one of the "ugliest of the
children of men."

The other line of thought stemmed from Psalm 45:2
"You are the fairest of the sons of men." This line of
thought painted Jesus in words and in pictures in the
beauty of the Olympian gods.
—*William Barclay,* The Mind of Jesus

43

MEDITATION

"Jesus, I wonder, what did you look like?
Is your appearance part of my attraction for you?"

Open to a few Gospel scenes at random. Preaching, healing, confronting, praying, traveling, eating, feeling stress. . . . Then as an exercise in imaginative prayer try to imagine Jesus' physical appearance in one of these scenes as if you were an artist. Sketch Him in detail—eyes, height, build, skin, face, etc. Approach Jesus in that scene. Ask about the matter of physical appearance, His and yours. Would it matter if He were beautiful, plain, or ugly? How?

To stir further thought see Matthew 6:28-34. "As for clothes, why be concerned. . . . Stop worrying, then, over questions such as, "What are we to eat, or what are we to drink, or what are we to wear. . . ." What are the fullest meanings you can find in these words?

SEEDS

Open a Gospel at random again and allow yourself to remain in questioning and wonder, enjoyment and awe, that God would so "empty Himself" for you and for me that we could see, touch, hear, and love. Does it seem unbelievably gladdening that God Himself took flesh so much like yours and mine that Jesus would wake in the morning, use whatever bathroom there was, put on sandals and clothes, and perhaps select from His presumably meager wardrobe? (Tell Him so.)

Do you ever worry about your looks and then get envious or critical of others? Can you be glad you are you? Because your unique body and your appearance are the special ones He would like for walking about in today's world. Yours!

Broken people have special beauty that Jesus recognized. When we can recognize that beauty too, we have become more like Him.

Could you be more sensitive today to someone other people don't seem to appreciate? Or pray for someone who doesn't seem to appreciate himself/herself?

Do I find myself making assumptions about persons based on skin colors or facial characteristics?

Babies—who can resist their appearance or smiles? And what strength and devotion can appear in an older person's face!

A smile can beautify anyone. I wonder whether Jesus smiled.

Human beauty, like all beauty, reflects the glory of God and can be highly helpful to Jesus' work. Do the ads and media offer us the truth about human beauty?

Handicaps can be blessings or curses. And attitude is what makes the difference.

What part does physical attraction play in my dealings with others? What if it played more . . . or less?

MEDITATION

2

PERSONALITY

More important than physical appearance is the kind of person one is, the assembling of qualities and traits we call personality. Which brings us to: What kind of person was Jesus?

Among the Evangelists, Saint Mark in particular has no scruples about presenting the wholly human Jesus with a full range of human emotions and even gestures:

> Jesus is carpenter 6:3
> asking questions which could imply ignorance 6:38, 9:16
> declaring he doesn't know the day the world will end 13:22
> angry at hardness of heart 3:5
> contradicting some quite bluntly ("you are wrong") 12:27
> sighing in disappointment or sympathy 8:12
> moved with compassion 6:34
> surprised at rejection in his home town 6:5-6
> looking with real affection on the rich young man 10:21
> marveling at unbelief 6:6
> feeling hunger 11:12
> feeling tired 6:31 even asleep in a storm 5:38
> frustrated in trying to escape the crowd 7:24
> lonely on the way to the passion 10:32
> greatly disturbed in Gethsemane 14:34
> —*Thomas Kealy, CSSP,* Who Is Jesus of
> Nazareth?

He was also approachable with people, gentle with women, enjoyed children, and held crowds spellbound. People felt deep affection for Him. And twelve contemporary men from various backgrounds made decisions to sign up with Him even before His resurrection!

MEDITATION

About Jesus' personality . . . what was He like, what kind of person was He?

Open the Gospels at random a few times, or select a few texts from the above. From those texts what do you think Jesus was like? How would you describe Him? What does each text add to your impression? Talk with Jesus as moved. (This is a meditation you could easily repeat.)

SEEDS

The way you look at yourself and feel about yourself depends a lot on how others react to you. How do you think you strike others? With a little thought and a little practice, could you become (still more than you already are, of course!) One Very Gracious and Personable Human Being?

"The glory of God is man fully alive."
—*St. Irenaeus*

The good points about me are . . .

Some untapped possibilities in me are . . .

How do you get along with people quite different from yourself? How do they get along with you? "To love" is an art that can be learned, as is the ability to relate well.

How do you handle criticism, coolness, being ignored or rejected? Are you inclined to withdraw, pout, strike out, overdrink . . . ? If so, ask Jesus, to help you find some better way. . . .

Are you all tied up with pleasing everyone, or always being a success, or keeping up this or that appearance, so it's hard to feel free, relaxed, and yourself? Sit down with Jesus, and talk it all through.

Can you appreciate another's differences in terms of what that person means to you and you to them?

Sometimes in sickness or old age, one's personality may seem to change. This can be hard to bear for the ill and the nurses alike. "Jesus, if I need help to bear this cross, whether as carer or cared-for, be with me!" In the Cross of Jesus is Power. In the Cross accepted is peace.

Pray for or talk with Jesus about someone you have noticed who seems to have difficulty relating to others.

Jesus, what am I to do about relatives, groups or even nationalities I find it hard to stomach? And what's to be done about nationalities who can't stomach one another?

Loving is an art, and arts can be learned.

MEDITATION

3

MAKING DECISIONS

Besides concern for appearance and personality, another easy topic for intimate conversation with Jesus is this: "What shall I do?" Many persons find themselves torn, now and then, about making decisions. For Jesus, too, not everything was clear and all preprogrammed. Scripture gives evidence that Jesus struggled to find His identity and how to carry on His Father's work in the same way as you and I.

Such struggle is exceptionally evident in the Desert Temptations. Having received from His Father *some* kind of communication about His mission regarding the Kingdom, He secluded Himself to pray, to try to decide how to go about it. His commission was to start a world movement of forgiveness, healing, care, and concern for the least as well as the great. Should He use military force, or a great display of powerful miracles to establish Israel as a temporal power? Israel could then gain the respect of the world and bring to other nations His Father's message. Or should He use only gentle and nonviolent means, without such miracles? Since He would be open to intense and even bitter opposition, would not such gentle means be rather foolish, even though indicated by the Father?

MEDITATION

On what basis did Jesus make choices and decisions? "Jesus, what was the bottom line?"

Read Matthew 4:1-14*

Then talk with the Lord about what is happening—about the wrestlings, the inner temptations and tensions. Try to feel with Him the strong pull to use miraculous powers to establish Himself as King. How else could He keep followers? Why not make stones into bread, and feed hungry crowds? Why not make some spectacular leap to show that God would save Him?

Sit on a rock, or in some cave-shelter by His side. Let Him tell you about it. In your prayer, try to experience with Him His striving. His struggle to accept God's will is what the Temptation scene in Jesus' life is all about.

> *(Matthew)
> *Jesus was led into the desert to be tempted . . . to make stones into bread, to leap from the parapet, to adore Satan and be given the world. "Away, Satan!"*

SEEDS

"Why do I do as I do?"

The underlying motive for many of my ordinary decisions is apt to be . . . (This is one searching question!)

Do you think you pre-plan life, or that in most things you flow with What Comes? Each way is appropriate at certain times.

Do you think you live somewhat conscious of your motivation, or that in most things you just do what should be done without thinking much about it?

It's a great art to handle youself well after making a bad

choice, or after doing something you regret. "Lord, what would you suggest? Especially if the hurting feelings hang on and on as they are prone to."

Added Thoughts for Long-Term Pondering

Little by little, we try to make the Best Motives our real motives. But it's a struggle. However, there is something OK about mixed motives, such as donating to charity and getting a tax write-off at the same time. Barring sinful intentions, let not fear of mixed motives prevent good work.

Notice how one of the main life-goals presented by the media is to live almost SOLELY for enjoyment. Money, Prestige, and Power are front-runners, too. For others, having someone to love who will love them back is The Whole of Life. How would you comment?

To live a life principally for pleasure is destructive. But to let pleasure in, to feel it and rejoice while you are doing something worth while is healthy and Christian. You accept pleasure, enjoy it, and give thanks, rather than concentrate on obtaining it as the main goal.

It is typical of Christian living to be seeking our Father's will—the loving thing to do—and not always to be sure of it. Keep seeking until it becomes clearer. It is also typical to be trying to do our Father's will, but not finding immediate or evident results. This is all right too. Jesus "had the same trouble."

If most people made their rule of life: "How much good can I do today?"—the world would be different in ways hard to imagine!

Are you able to take a strong, yet open and hope-filled stance on a well-founded conviction, when others see it from a different viewpoint—as for example regarding the Church's teaching on peace?

Am I aware of how my small daily choices *can* help impact others in long-term ways, for example by refusing to buy from companies with unjust labor practices or humanly harmful marketing policies; or by how much wealth I accumulate and what I do with it?

MEDITATION

4

JESUS AS A PERSON

Everyone knows Jesus was divine. All through history it has been necessary to stress this. But sometimes, in different periods, Jesus' humanity has been eclipsed. People have become afraid to come near and to accept the very thing He came to offer: His human friendship.

For example, in the early 1900's people were often afraid to receive Communion more than once a year, and then only because it was obligatory. People prayed more to Mary, and felt closer to Mary and the saints than to Jesus. Part of this neglect was due to thinking of Jesus as so awesomely divine that He was not really approachable as human.

Another reason for neglect of His human side was that people thought Jesus enjoyed the Beatific Vision so fully from the beginning of His life that His whole life was already arranged—programmed in every detail like a puppet's on a string. It was thought He never had to go through the agony of decisions as we do because his life was simply following an already written script.

The consensus of modern theologians and Scripture scholars is with Karl Rahner, that Jesus' knowledge of Himself as divine was not reflexively (consciously) conscious before the time of His resurrection. That is, He was not consciously aware of His divinity, even though there may have been present a kind of background knowledge to that effect. And neither were His Father's designs always revealed in every detail. If they were, why did He pray "My God, My God, why have You forsaken Me?" Or pray in the garden, "*If* it be Your will" (implying a lack of certain knowledge), or "Let this chalice pass from Me," or pray before all major decisions? Why did He say clearly that He did not know when the world would end, or ask "Who touched Me?" or "Why do you ask Me?" and other such questions as Scripture records.

We do not like to think Jesus was just play-acting for our benefit, or that these experiences and questions were really not His true questions or experiences. That would come dangerously close to Jesus' deceiving us.

Such reflections as the above can be very comforting. They mean that Jesus really can understand our human condition and *feel* for us. He went through joys and sorrows similar to ours. Several times He was in darkness over everyday matters, much as we are. As St. Paul says, "Jesus was like us in *all things but sin*." So He was like us in *limited* knowledge, at least in some matters. This point will be new to some, so let us sum up by saying that: the theory that Jesus possessed the Beatific Vision consciously from the beginning of His life was a theory of St. Thomas, and only a theory. This theory is now being superseded often (thought not necessarily always) by the older, more "human" emphasis reflected in some Fathers of the Church such as St. Cyril of Alexandria.

MEDITATION

Reflect as you will. Does Jesus seem really human to you? Are you relating as human to human? "Jesus, how do you see it between us?"

SEEDS

Do you feel comfortable with Human Jesus? Is being "comfortable" in a relationship something important?

"When I hear the name "Jesus" my first and spontaneous

feeling is likely to be . . . ." (What do you make of that reaction?)

Compose a very human, personal heartfelt prayer to Jesus. Let "heart speak to heart," expressing anything your deepest human self suggests—plus, minus, enthusiasm, apathy, conflict, or absence of feeling . . . whatever.

> And the Word
> became flesh . . .
> and pitched
> his tent
> among us!
> —*John 1:14*

How was Jesus' personality shaped by everyday living? By the political and social climate of his times?

MEDITATION

5

JOYS

People often seek out Jesus when they need help, or when they want light for decisions, or they are feeling Down. Why not also share the nice, the pleasant, the blessings and the highs?

"Jesus, did you ever share with your Father the joys of everyday living? Like what? Did you ever share the happiness you were feeling in good work done for Him, or pleasure in using your miraculous powers, or elation at being able to heal and announce your Father's love and care?"

MEDITATION

First, browse in Scripture for things you think He might have shared, and try to imagine, if you can, how He did.

Then, as part of this meditation, select a positive experience of your own and share it with Jesus. Relive an experience when you felt like shouting for joy, praising God, or were elated over music, and try to get the feel of sharing that with him. Or how about when you were enthusiastic over a hobby, or feeling the joy of sex, food, drink, or winning a game?

Do you remember when you got that promotion? Or what of the simple pleasure of contemplating art, or the wonder in a child's face at a surprise? How about jogging, partying, a friend's loyalty, being complimented, or owning the winning lottery number?

It may be a new experience to share pleasant things. But never doubt that intimacy over joys goes with His invitation to walk closer. You are not imposing. "I have called you friends." It will be Joy that we share for all eternity. So just for practice now, share some Plus Experience, something tingling with excitement or something quiet.

SEEDS

Some Scripture writers think Jesus may have thoroughly enjoyed using His power over the storm at sea!

How do you think Jesus reacted to the ordinary humor-filled incongruities that crowd into every life? "Do you remember when . . . !?"

Is this a day to brighten someone's life by affirming, lightening the burden, or just a good word to notice they exist? Or by writing or phoning? Everyone can do *something*! Live long so you can do much!

It helps life to wake up in the morning and start Positive Thinking. It is even better to start Positive Noticing as to how God might want to reach out and love you today.

What kinds of pleasures deserve greater emphasis in our days?

"Jesus I wonder, did you ever go out for an evening with your friends? What DID you do for Rest and Relaxation?"

If Jesus' people, redeemed, forgiven, and loved seem always sad or sour-looking, what's happening?

Vatican II calls us to make the joys and hopes of the human family our own. Are there things going on about which you and Jesus can rejoice together?

MEDITATION

6

SORROWS

Do you ever feel disappointed or as if you aren't getting anywhere? Or wonder whether there must be more to life than 9 to 5, or housework? Or if anyone cares? Or whether it all makes any difference? Do you just seem to have so many everyday worries? Jesus had these too. He also died with many plans and dreams unrealized . . . as so many of us do.

MEDITATION

"What was it like for you Lord—the everyday stress?" (Read Mark 3:7-10 and 20.*) "How did you manage yourself? What kept you going?"

For more, try to enter His heart and sense the frustration close to the *beginning* of His work, as in Matthew 9:36-37*. See also Matthew 23:27* for the same thing toward the *end* of His life. So many were in need of His strength and help. His work was to be worldwide, but with only one or three years to accomplish it. Share His joy in the good already done, yet feel with Him how it is tempered with the ever-anxious wish for More and Faster. He seems always pressured. Even harried. "The time is short," he keeps saying over and over.

> *(Mark)
> *Jesus ordered a fishing boat ready so they could avoid
> the press of the crowd . . . all who had afflictions kept*

*pushing toward him to touch him . . . the crowd
assembled making it impossible to get any food
whatever.*

*(Matthew 9)
At the sight of the crowds his heart was moved with
pity. They were lying prostrate from exhaustion, like
sheep without a shepherd. He said to his disciples:
"The harvest is good, but the laborers are scarce...."*

*(Matthew 23)
Jerusalem, Jerusalem . . . how often have I yearned to
gather your children, as a mother bird gathers her young
under her wings, but you refused me."*

SEEDS

Jesus, did you ever have Blue Mondays?

Is there some unresolved worry or pain with which you just
have to plod on? "Am I getting old or ill, or can I keep food
on the table, or will I find someone to love or marry me, or is
there help for my problem, or will anyone push my
wheelchair?"

Failures, those are the hard ones. You try, you plan, you sweat,
and it just doesn't work out regarding money, business, love,
the children, sports, studies, health, you name it. Jesus had
everyday failures too. You can bring yours to Him knowing
He will understand. From experience.

Fatigue, stress, overwork, the pace too fast? Feeling not
appreciated . . . ? "Jesus, what shall we do about these

situations?" Go on the assumption that usually something can be done about almost any problem, or about your attitude, or about both.

If you are just plain weary, read John 4:6 and Mark 6:31, and hear Jesus saying: "Come to me you who labor and are heavily burdened. I will refresh you." Let Him do so in any way you imagine. Sense it happening. He is cradling, loving, comforting, lifting the weight, bringing you peace.

Hurt feelings from humiliations and from rejected love are some of the worst hurts of all.

Will God, Jesus, and religion be helpful to relaxing and finding life good? Probably. Are they intended to be? Undoubtedly!

> Pray for someone
> under stress,
> or for some harried group.

Lord, I feel sorrow and frustration at the immensity of social problems, and the great difficultly of making even the smallest impact towards a world where the basic rights of each person are respected.

Do we need in Christian people more sadness in prayer like to Jesus' weeping over Jerusalem?

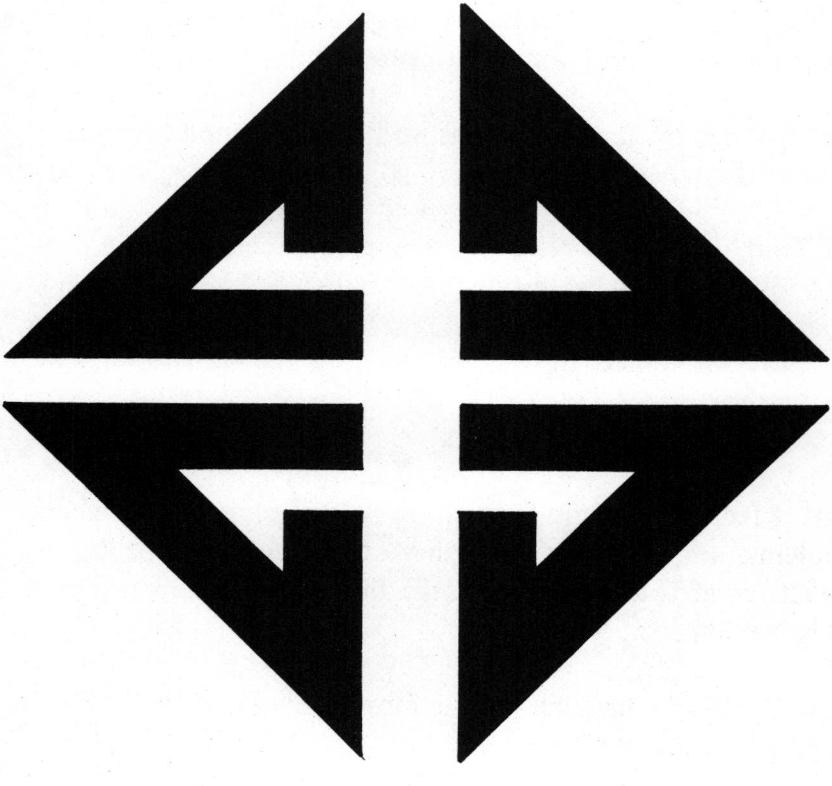

MEDITATION

7

MY NEGATIVE SELF

This is a prayer experience about admitting (or is it not admitting?) Jesus to the Dark Side. So often we do not.

MEDITATION

With some hesitation I ask . . . but maybe it's all for the best. . . . where would you like entrance to my life, Jesus, in these darker areas? See Luke 15:11-19* and/or Psalm 51*.

Suggestion:
Take any area of sin, darkness, or negative feeling toward God, people or self, or any reluctance to love and live for Jesus, and just open it up. Lay it on the line. You needn't make a decision about the matter during this meditation, should you prefer not to. Just bring it out into the open so there can at least be communication about the matter. Where would Jesus like entrance with his healing help?

Talk with him about what it's like to have the problem. Include that "communicating" may be a problem itself. Try to know and feel deeply that Jesus understands. This matter *is* a problem and struggle for you, isn't it? He wants to help heal, to free, and to forgive if needed. He understands your problems; and He loves to hear that *you know* that He understands.

*(Luke 15)
*Coming to his senses at last, he said, "How many
hired hands at my father's place have more than
enough to eat, while here I am starving. I will break
away and return to my father and say to him, 'Father
I have sinned . . . .'"*

*(Psalm 51)
I acknowledge my offense . . . .

SEEDS

Some samples of what we are talking about: The sense of
being angry at God for having to face life alone; being
disloyal to people we love; disappointment at prayers not
answered; frustration at lack of freedom; fretting over a
personal relationship that has soured; temptation toward
greed, inappropriate sex, selfishness, drugs, flirtatiousness,
drink; lack of care about health, spouse or family; or just
plain brooding.

> You honor Jesus by bringing Him into the "dark side"
> of your life. That is where He wants to be. Calvary
> was his price of admission . . . .
> —*John B. Healey*

A friend is one who knows you just as you are and loves you
anyway.

In sharing matters like this there is only so much Jesus can do.
He can invite sharing . . . . A burden shared is a burden
halved.

If sharing is uncomfortable, it might draw you and the Lord closer to tell him so.

Have others ever mentioned to you some struggle in their quest for Jesus? If so, pray for them.

Many times we have difficulty even seeing those dark parts of ourselves. Clues can be gotten from things we dislike or find especially annoying or disturbing in other individuals, or in people of other social groups. Very often these strong reactions indicate part of ourselves that we fear or are not seeing or accepting. Thus, loving oneself and loving one's enemies are closely related.

MEDITATION

8

SEXUALITY

Sexuality is an energizing and all-pervasive area of human living that deserves "equal time" with other topics in relating to the Lord.

Essay on Sexuality

"It is helpful for people to present themsevles honestly before the Lord, in all their joy and happiness, as well as in their confusion, doubts, or turmoil, if such be present, regarding matters sexual. People may never have spoken openly to the Lord about their sexual desires and fantasies, except to confess them as sinful. They may be reluctant to do so. There is the reluctance to speak about such intimate aspects of oneself to anyone, including God. Moreover, most of us have feelings of shame connected with sexuality. Finally, reluctance can arise because we are afraid of God's reaction to our sexuality. We fear that He may be angry at us for having sexual desires, or that He will make demands on us that we do not want to face. People in love may fear that He will demand that they give one another up. In our Christian training God has not been presented as friendly toward sexuality, except within very strict limits. Thus people need help to present themselves honestly before God.

"If a person does begin, however tentatively, to tell the Lord what is happening to him and how he or she is reacting, what occurs? He or she is often surprised to discover that the Lord does not seem to be angry at him or her, that, in fact, He is understanding and consoling.

"Perhaps for the first time he learned that he can speak the truth about his sexuality to God, and that God is not scandalized, as it were. He is then encouraged by such experiences to be more and more open in prayer. He tells the Lord about the fantasies, the strong desires, the imperiousness of his arousal states. He may well find that, with the telling, the pressure abates somewhat; he is less a hapless victim of his passion, and more in control of himself.

"Within him a transformation takes place. He gradually is being freed of negative attitudes toward his body and his sexuality, and toward sexuality in general. Some of this change can be attributed to the fact that he loves and is loved by another. But the change in attitude also occurs because he finds that the Lord is not only tolerant of him as a sexual being, but is with him in the struggle with his sexuality as He is in all his struggles. Jesus understands because He Himself was a sexual human being."
—*William Barry, S.J.*

MEDITATION

Can you let Jesus into the sexual areas of your life: love, romance, physical attraction? "Jesus, this is how I am." Or could you let yourself and Jesus work out your sexual self at your best?

"How would you see me, Lord, as a sexually gifted person?"

What are the advantages of being gifted as sexual as part of your total person? Aren't you glad you are?

Sexuality is intended as an energizing way of being, not a burden; a constructive drive, not a problem; a part of a total person, and not an end in itself.

"God created man in his image, male and female . . . God looked at everything he made and he found it very good."
—*Genesis 1.*

The old idea that sex is bad, in itself wicked, in itself dirty, etc., cannot be correct by Biblical standards.

"Sometimes I feel sexy and romantic toward persons I haven't the right to get sexy and romantic about. Then what, Lord?"

Any comments with Jesus about sex vis-a-vis our times? Is something beautiful and intended to be richly meaningful (the full meaning of sexual attraction between men and women) being trivialized? For example, "Sex without love."

Remember that sexuality is much more than genitality. Qualities that are called masculine, i.e., strength, power, activity, analysis and rationality, as well as those termed feminine such as receptivity, tenderness, gentleness, nurturing and compassion must be present in the mature person of either sex. How were those two sets of qualities present in Jesus?

Unless we accept our need to develop both facets in ourselves we can easily end up asking another person to supply a missing part of ourselves. That is an impossible burden for anyone to

68

take on, or to have put on them. A better way is to recognize our need to grow into mature personhood and to learn from each other. One of the biggest problems of our world today is that our social, national and international relations are built too one-sidedly on so-called masculine characteristics. A most striking example is Nazi Germany. The more feminine aspects of caring and compassion must come into play before we can ever solve problems of political oppression or world hunger. The full acceptance of our own sexuality and of our respective sexual relations with others is important to more than ourselves.

MEDITATION

9

COMPASSION

First, an imaginative scene. It is some time after the Creation of Humankind. The Father, Son, and Spirit brood over the world, intended to be radiant and beautiful, now so filled with deceit, broken trust, and cruelty. "What is to be done?" they ask themselves. (One wonders what they are thinking. Are they seeing that, left to themselves, humans would surely destroy one another?)

The Son, with a Compassion that is His Father's own, volunteers to come and save us. The Father assents. So Jesus takes flesh, touches, and heals. He mends lepers' sores, mourns over the Jerusalem that would not come to Him, lets it be known in a thousand ways that God our Father loves us still. In Jesus, God takes children in His arms and in this gesture He cradles the ungoverned and fear-filled children in us all. He caresses, blesses, and encourages us to be gentle with ourselves and with others as a way of life. Jesus would like to share with us this astounding, heartening fact: His Father is Compassion. We are saying this because it is so important: Jesus' Father and ours *is* Compassion.

MEDITATION

How do you usually think about or feel toward God? Read Luke 15:19-31*. Then reflect or speak to the Father as you feel moved.

*(Luke)
While he was still a long way off, his father caught sight of him and was deeply moved. He ran out to meet him, threw his arms around his neck and kissed him. The son said to him, "Father, I have sinned against God and against you; I no longer deserve to be called your son." The father said to his servants: "Quick! Bring the finest robe. . . ."

SEEDS

Do you think most people sense our Father as gentle, loving, and forgiving? That He is not irate and eager to punish, contrary to the impression the Old Testament sometimes gives? We are in the New Covenant of mercy, meaning gracious and forgiving loving-kindness. Do you sense that you may call him Abba, Papa, Daddy, Father? That he is interested in everything about you and about your life? And He so much wants to have children whom he can enjoy being around forever. That's why he made so many of us.

Because of the Father's compassion, you can be compassionate to *any*one, even if your love is rejected. So you could go about today showing more than ordinary compassion for just everyone—because *you* are endlessly loved and *given* compassion.

"Jesus, as I think or pray about this, what are you saying to me personally about our Father?"

The next time you pick up the daily paper, notice: Who or what is crying for compassion? What do you think is the

Father's reaction to what you see on the front page? You might want to make your prayer to cry out with Jesus: "Father, forgive." God loves us as fathers do and as mothers do; and mothers, happily, love us as we are!

The Toys

My little Son, who look'd from
thoughtful eyes and moved and
spoke in quiet grown-up wise,
Having my law the seventh time
disobey'd, I struck him, and
dismiss'd With hard words and
unkiss'd,—His mother, who was
patient, being dead. Then,
fearing lest his grief should
hinder sleep, I visited his bed,
But found him slumbering deep,
With darken'd eyelids, and their
lashes yet from his late sobbing wet.
And I, with moan,
Kissing away his tears, left others of
my own; For on a table drawn beside his
head, he had put, within his reach, A box
of counters and a red-vein'd stone,
A piece of glass abraded by the beach
And six or seven shells,
A bottle with bluebells,
And two French copper coins, ranged there with
careful art,
To comfort his sad heart.
So when that night I pray'd
To God, I wept, and said:

Ah, when at last we lie with tranced breath,
Not vexing Thee in death,
And thou rememberest of what toys
We made our joys,
How weakly understood,
Thy great commanded good,
Then, fatherly not less
Than I whom thou hast moulded from the clay,
Thou'lt leave thy wrath, and say,
"I will be sorry for their childishness."
　　　—*Coventry Patmore*

Be gentle and compassionate to your faults: "Come now, my soul, we can do better." (St. Francis de Sales' advice.) You'll get
further.

To the extent we share the Father's compassion for all humankind we will find it increasingly important to be concerned with the causes of suffering which the Church so strongly calls us to do.

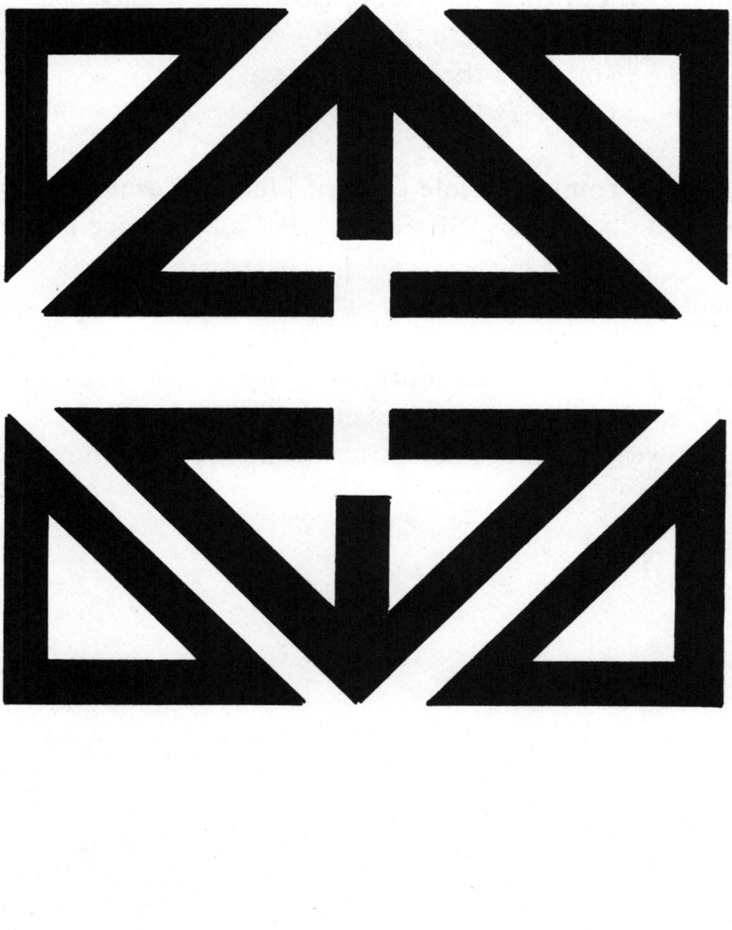

MEDITATION

10

EVERYDAY LIFE

Jesus must have been in close contact with everyday things. His parables in particular are so full of salt, yeast, weather, one thousand kinds of human behavior; innkeepers and thieves, good widows and harlots, seeds and sunshine, fishermen and shepherds. What more natural topic to talk about with his Father? Even when quite young He must have been open to the talk of the times because Nazareth was on commercial routes between Asia and Egypt and He may well have gotten quite an earful from traveling merchants.

MEDITATION

As an exercise in prayer, try to imagine how the young Jesus might have taken some of the news about current events or people to His Father in prayer. Or try to imagine how He might have done that with something from His public life.

Then try to do the same. Take people or events in your life to Jesus. Then to the Father. A child's success, a plane crash, a loving deed, a relative or friend, an international confrontation—anything or everything is material for prayer. Include as possibilities the joys of the day, the reading you are doing, the music you listen to.

Pray about some person who really matters to you. Pray that their strengths increase and their weaknesses be healed. You could also pray about how well you relate.

Hostile feelings? It helps to remember in prayer: those other people may be the way they are for some good reason that we simply do not know. And secondly, do we really have to react with hostility if we prefer not to? Can't we choose to react some other way?

Pray for someone in a difficult family situation; or about the death of a friend and how Jesus felt at Lazarus' death. Sometimes you can match people and events in your life with similar situations in His.

Pray over the trends of the times, escalating crime or divorce, growth of drugs or erotica, and for increased success of some wholesome life-giving trend.

Pray about your relationship with Jesus.

Jesus really loves individuals. At Lazarus' death Jesus began to weep which caused the Jews to remark "See how much he loved him!"

People in prisons or nursing homes who feel cast off and forgotten by our social world—is there some way I can help them to know Jesus cares for them too?

There is hardly any area of living more prominent, more close to our thoughts than *people*. Indeed, as Martin Buber said:

Living is meeting. In our age in particular, the note of intimacy
with people ranks high if not highest on the list of things that
provide our pleasure and pain. It's the people in our lives,
including Jesus, that so much make us who we are, comfort
and strengthen, bring out the best in us as well as the worst,
that so much wrap up what the Gospel is about.

Each person is a struggling seed, a fragile package, whom God
is luring to himself, though they may not realize it.

So many people have brought good to our lives. We will want
to pray in gratitude for blessings for them.

RELAXING AS AN AID TO PRAYER

In spite of the vigor of His life and His strenuous battles against evil, there can be no doubt: Jesus was a peace-loving person. And one of the most helpful dispositions, so as to enjoy His peace in prayer, is to feel peaceful and relaxed physically. So, this is a brief instruction about relaxation as an aid to meditating and following Jesus—in peace, as a peace-bringing person.

"Your muscles are taut. In order to relax, you must slow that motor down. Begin by telling yourself that you will relax, then follow this step-by-step program.

(1) Start by loosening your clothing or removing any that fit too snugly.

(2) Now lie down and begin slowing down your breathing. At the height of tension, your breath may be coming in short, quick gasps. Breathe deeply and exhale slowly for a few minutes. Then increase the time interval between these deep breaths. In a few minutes, start breathing less deeply, but still at the lengthened time interval. Your body motor should be slowing down.

(3) It's time to drain the tension out of your body. You start this by creating a little extra tension, strange though that may seem. Concentrate on your legs first. Tense your muscles as much as you possibly can. Hold that state of tension for a second or two. Then gradually, slowly relax, little by little. Continue until you have drained every last ounce of tension out of your legs.

(4) Now that your legs are in a relaxed state, move on

to your abdomen and chest. Repeat the tensing and slow relaxation process with these areas until the last bit of tension is wrung out.

(5) Now tense your arms as tightly as you can. Gradually relax them. Follow this same procedure until they lie limp at your sides.

(6) Your neck and head are next. Tense them as you did the other parts of your body. Then give them the slow, tension-draining routine until they feel heavy and completely relaxed.

NOTE: At this point your body motor should be running at a very low idle. If you still feel tense, repeat the step-by-step program.

More Soothing Suggestions

You may find more relaxation by 'escaping' into a soothing environment. Try taking a long walk at a rapid pace. This helps to use up nervous energy. At home, try a comfortable warm bath or shower. Write a letter. Read a book. Meditate!

Emotionally, conjure up a vision of yourself feeling calm, relaxed, soothed. Picture yourself in a soothing environment as you lie down. Let your thoughts drift into images of pleasure and delight. Let your mind dwell on pleasant visions and memories. It can do much to help you relax. You will find yourself drifting off into a state of relaxed contentment."
—*National Health Bulletin*

So—before beginning to meditate get relaxed, expecting to enjoy what you are about to do.

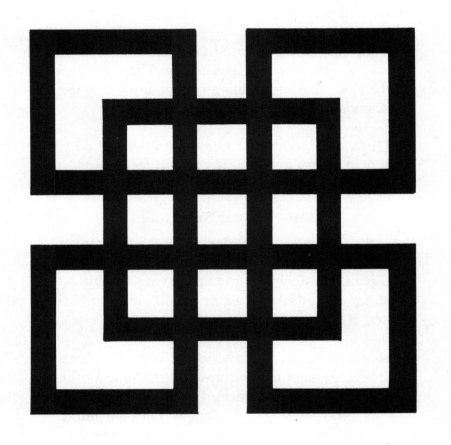

CHAPTER THREE

GROWING IN PRAYER

INTRODUCTION

SHARING A DREAM

Intimacy with Jesus, that is what we are about in these meditations. But intimacy means more than just communicating over everyday matters, as in the last chapter. We want also to sense "what makes Him go." What are His hopes, fears, central concerns? What are His ambitions, deep motives, His dreams. . . ?

Happiness, romance, fulfillment, money, friends—we all have dreams. What is life without them? But sometimes a person has One Special Dream. Jesus was that kind of person, and we are about to enter that one special dream with Him.

Reminder of Meditation Guides

Begin a meditation in the Presence of God. Or sit in a chair next to Jesus!

Then read the meditation and the Scripture as if the Spirit inspired its writing just for you! Read slowly and thoughtfully. Pause to listen* for *your* reaction. Pray over it till it runs dry. Then, if you wish, begin conversation or praise or thanks or mulling over anything else that strikes you. Express *any* feeling, perhaps in short, repeated phrases, "How lovely your dream, O Lord!" Each meditation is apt to offer several ideas, or feelings, or applications, but it is preferable to select just one and stay with it.

If after waiting for a while and listening, nothing seems to come, re-read aloud, slowly, from the beginning. Pause immediately whenever you find a feeling of peace, an insight, or some attraction. Stay with it as long as it seems useful.

Conclude with a short heart-to-heart time with the Lord. Don't hassle yourself about the length of the Meditation.

If it's one of those days when nothing works, read a few Psalms to fill out the time, or Scripture, or a spiritual book, pausing if moved. If terribly distracted, make THAT the subject for being with the Lord.

*To "listen" means: try to become aware of whether you get a thought or feeling or impulse to act— any reaction. It may take a while to become aware. "What are you saying Lord? What am I feeling?"

MEDITATION

1

THE KINGDOM OF GOD

I dream of things that never were, and say: Why not?"
  —*G.B. Shaw*

A modern proposal of some features of God's Reign of Love on earth could be the following:

Every child (every living person)
is entitled to affection, love and understanding;
to adequate nutrition and medical care;
to a free education;
to the opportunity for play and recreation;
to a name and nationality;
to special care if handicapped;
to have a chance to become a useful member of
society;
and to develop individual abilities;
to live in peace and universal brotherhood;
and to the enjoyment of these rights regardless of
      race,
color, sex, religion, national or social origins.
    —*Adapted from United Nations statement on
      Rights of Children*

A more personal statement of Jesus' dream:

> I dream a world where man
> No other will scorn,
> Where love will bless the earth
> And peace its paths adorn.
> I dream a world where all
> Will know sweet freedom's way,
> Where greed no longer saps the soul
> Nor avarice blights our day.
> A world I dream where black or white,
> Whatever race you be,
> Will share the bounties of the earth
> And every man is free,
> Where wretchedness will hang its head,
> And joy, like a pearl,
> Attend the needs of all mankind.
> Of such I dream—
> Our world!
> —*Langston Hughes*

MEDITATION

What is Jesus' Dream? Let Him tell you about it. For some of His own words, see Matthew 13:44-46*. And for a beautifully poetic statement see Isaiah 65:17-25* and Micah 4:1-5*.

For Jesus to proclaim the Kingdom meant: To proclaim that God's Love and Power are bursting into history, NOW! God's love and power are entering the world afresh to help and heal our wounded natures, to confront and heal all evil and sin, to help us become Better People in a Better World, to reestablish God's claims to our love and devotion, to being First in our lives. It is beginnings of Paradise again; peace, love, justice, harmony . . . .

Spend one or more days on this marvelous world-vision and all it implies until you feel your heart glowing with it. The Kingdom is the central passion, desire, integrating ideal, and energizing force behind all that Jesus said and did. Basically, it means everyone living to love God and each other under Jesus' Headship. Sometimes it is called: My Father's Kingdom. Sometimes Jesus' Kingdom.

*(Matthew)
The reign of God is like a buried treasure . . . or one really valuable pearl.

*(Isaiah)
Lo, I am about to create a new heaven and a new earth . . . there will be rejoicing . . . no sound of crying . . . and the wolf and the lamb shall graze alike.

*(Micah)
They shall beat their swords into plowshares . . . nor shall they ever train for war again . . . every man shall sit under his own vine or under his own fig tree undisturbed.

SEEDS

Consider the practical advantages, indeed the excitement of, first, having a central life-view; and then of making the Kingdom that life-view. (Keep Jesus in the picture!)

More than working for a Shangri-La, Camelot, Utopia, or Great Society, working for the Kingdom involves a relationship with Jesus. Only in Him lies even the possibility of Shalom, peace and harmony of people with one another, nature, and God that we all dream of and so want for others as well as ourselves.

Everything you do or suffer can be for some very good reason, to leave yourself or others a little happier or better today. *Jesus' Kingdom!*—You can almost feel it in your bones—It cries out, "*Life has meaning*! Today I can love and serve Jesus. I want to crowd my life with all the goodness I can, while I have the time and energy."

As a prayer experiment, try "Giving Yourself Away," taking advantage of almost every single opportunity to say a good word or do a kind deed for one whole day of each week. The rewards and spinoffs can be remarkably gratifying.

Try to imagine a typical day in different occupations for people who take "Thy Kingdom come" for the real passion of their lives.

> "You do what you can, OK?
> I'll do the rest."
> —*Jesus*

MEDITATION

2

EVIL

Against Christ's Reign of Love (and so, against our happiness and well-being) there is an all-too-real and contrary Force. Two totally dedicated life-views are pulling in opposite directions.

If you look around, you will see it happening:
the everlasting battle between Better Self and Wounded Self,
between living solely for me and sharing with others,
between the impulse to trust and impulse to exploit,
between the gentle sector of us and the violent,
between the pure and the pornographic,
between struggling for the common good,
    and grabbing or dominating—regardless.
In short, it is the battle between Christ and Satan,
    between Good and Evil, All Good and All Evil.
It rages in everyone, everywhere . . . the War of the Two Kingdoms.

MEDITATION

Opposition to Jesus' Kingdom: who is involved; what is happening; why, where, when does it show itself? "Jesus, how do you see it?"

Read Romans 7:15-25* and 1 Peter 5-8*. For your meditation, after sitting with Jesus for a while and perhaps confusedly wondering at the human condition, pick up a newspaper. Notice the battle between good and evil behind the news on almost every page. Plan, as part of your meditation, to be observing it on TV at national and international levels. Plan to watch how it operates at places of business, school, home, and recreation. "Lord, is this see-saw battle what is *really* behind people's actions? In their hearts? in myself?"

Plan to take these matters to Jesus now and then for a few seconds during the day whenever you think about it.

> *(Romans)
> *I cannot even understand my own action. I do not do what I want but what I hate . . . I see in my body's members another law at war with the law of my mind . . . what a wretched man I am.*
>
> *(Peter)
> *. . . your adversary, the devil, goes about seeking whom he may devour.*

SEEDS

Behind all struggles: those of world history and my personal history, is usually . . . The War!

Jesus came to help us win The War, and we thank Him for that. However, life in its realism is: Some battles you win, some you lose. That's how it was for Jesus. "Jesus, give us courage to Hang In There when losing, as you did."

You could dramatize the foregoing meditation by picturing Christ, representing the forces of love and goodness, making an international TV appeal for help to win over the world. Then imagine Satan (Pride, etc.) making the same appeal on equal time. What would each say? In what dress would each appear? With what advantages or "come-ons" would each make his appeal? Put yourself in the audience. Are people being moved?

Is the world ever going to get better? Sometimes we can wonder if there *is* hope. Because "those who do not learn from the mistakes of the past are condemned to repeat them" (George Santayana). And that's what seems to keep happening. "So, Jesus, what shall we think?"

The War: Sometimes there are only two pieces of pie for three people, or scarce minerals among competing nations, or profit is struggling with human rights, or whatever.

"Jesus, I am such a war too, between what I ought to be doing and what I feel like doing. I wonder if others are like this. I'd like to be more understanding to others and myself too. Not indignant, not depressed over weakness. Compassionate."

"Jesus, life is such a struggle. I am glad you are near. Help me keep my balance, and trust, and sense of humor."

MEDITATION

3

IDEALS TO STRIVE TOWARD

We have seen Jesus' vision of life (Meditation 1), and Satan's or Evil's counter vision (Meditation 2). Now, how can ordinary people live in daily life in a loving way to help Jesus bring *His* view to prevail? Jesus said the First Thing to do was to "Repent" of doing evil, and then to try to do the Loving Thing as shown by such examples as:

> reconciliation rather than anger
> no compromise about their sins,
> commitment in marriage (faithfulness)
> being simple and direct of speech (honesty)
> being generous, even when generosity is taken
> advantage of,
> loving all equally, no matter who they are
> or what they have done,
> doing a lot of good, but not parading it,
> keeping motives pure (*Thy* Kingdom come, *Thy*
> will be done, instead of everything for me)
> simplicity of life-style,
> trusting the Father,
> praying for strength and other needs, and even
> willingness to suffer temporarily to bring about
> such a Kingdom.
> —*Adapted from* How to Read and Pray the Gospels
> *by Marilyn Norquist*

(These remarks summarize the Sermon on the Mount, Matthew Chapters 5, 6, and 7).

MEDITATION

Browse about in the Sermon, Matthew Chapters 5, 6, and 7. What are Kingdom people like? "Jesus, what are your people like? What is outstanding?"

If you like, see yourself at the scene: Where is it: Who is there? What is the setting? Are you standing or sitting? How does everyone look? What are they saying? What is Jesus saying? How are they reacting? How are you? These short questions help to open up any Scripture scene for contemplation.

SEEDS

If only the world were full of Kingdom-people . . . !

Read and ponder any part of the Sermon as if Jesus were saying these words straight to you. Invitingly. Which would you most treasure?

I can always have a positive self-image because I am always living to be part of and contributor to a Great Cause: My Father's Kingdom. I will therefore always have work of value to do, even if that be sometimes only suffering or failure. Yes, I can even hear in failure a call from God to bear with such circumstances. Like Jesus.

Consider how Sermon-people can best live their ideals in the world of today's business. Or at school. Or in politics. How do you stay consistently honest, or faithful, or generous when others around you are on the take? There are bound to be hassles, and sometimes the best we can do is to choose the lesser of two evils. "Be with us, Lord."

Kingdom does suggest Corporate Response. __Yes__No ("Corporate," meaning by any *large* group, including Church, business, or nation).

"Jesus, this all sounds great, but I am so weak."
"My daughter, my son, we all need stars to reach for. One step at a time, one step at a time."

SOME NOTES ABOUT MEDITATIONS 1-3

If the ideals of these meditations seem lofty,
well . . .
at least life can never be boring when reaching
for such as these!
However, one must not become guilt-laden for
not always succeeding, and perhaps hardly ever.

Rather, from these meditations let yourself
feel part of a great hope.
The most ordinary person, the most unnoticed
in the public eye, as well as the most prominent
and talented—each can do much.
All the more when a person supports an
enterprising Group Effort.

But, just simply as individuals,
each can make a great difference when
we do what we can.

We can pray,
We can bring Sermon principles to everyday life.
We can keep an eye to possibilities for wider influence.

We can write, phone, talk, read, prepare for
action, raise consciousness, love the
person nearby, and ourselves. We can get better
informed. Some can give money; and some even more of
their lives in volunteering. Those in positions of influence
can use that influence. Others can choose occupations or
vocations for the sake of the Kingdom. And everyone can
offer well-done daily tasks with deep faith for Jesus' work. It works!

Thus our efforts, aided by an enormous secret weapon,
The Power of God, can do whatever He wills.
We cannot do it alone, and
He has decided *not* to do it without us.

He wants to work right alongside—
in the Church, in Action Groups, and
with you and me as individuals.

We let Him lead. If the brush will
surrender to the painter, an incredibly
beautiful picture can emerge.
Indeed, the brush will wonder that such
grandeur was hidden within it!

Like Himself. I can always be about my
Father's business. *Always!*

MEDITATION

4

JESUS' PUBLIC LIFE

At this point, we join the crowds milling about Jesus to watch how He set His Grand Vision for our happiness into motion.

For each of the next three meditations read the passages in your Bible hand-in-hand with this commentary. As if you were present, observe in each incident how Jesus is concerned with inaugurating His New Reign of God, a Reign of Love. *Somehow* everything He does seems concerned with this goal. Try to observe how. Is He "overdoing" it?

Having observed, pause for a personal reflection or application after each passage, or after all three are completed.

Helpful questions to start your reflection: "Jesus, what are you thinking? What am I feeling? What does this mean?"

MEDITATIONS

a) *The Temptations*. Read Luke 4:1-13. Notice how Jesus rejects Satan's counter-Kingdom temptations: to found the Kingdom with a great show of pomp and display. Jesus is convinced that His Father wants it founded in a gentler way. "Love is gentle . . . ."

> Jesus, help me to turn away from pride or some other anti-Kingdom temptation. And Lord, they come on so strongly.

b) *Jesus at Nazareth.* Read Luke 4:14-32. Notice how Jesus makes a modest start on His Grand Enterprise (Kingdom) by reading Kingdom-Scriptures in the synagogue and declaring: "This prophecy is being fulfilled right before you. It's beginning right here and now."

> Jesus, include me into partnership. Show me how to help you*. Or help me get such a desire.

> If *I* wanted to start a Kingdom, I wonder what Scripture I would read?

*Only say this if you feel you can mean it. Being yourself is prayer's first requisite. Grow at your *pace* . . . .

c) *Cure of the Demoniac.* Read Luke 4:33-37. Notice how Jesus begins to show signs of God's power against the forces of Evil that oppose His Better World. He's breaking in with new Power.

> Jesus, cure my paralysis . . . whatever is hindering my dreaming with you. (Or pray similarly for someone else.)

> "Begone, evil demon, in Jesus' name." Or, "Inner weakness, in Jesus' name be healed."

Conclusion: What impression of Jesus are you getting? Did *any*thing in the above strike you for deeper prayer or application—to yourself, to other people, the times, or to all Jesus' followers? For example, does it strike you as interesting that Jesus begins His work with outcasts?

PRAYER HELPERS

> An excellent way to open up a Scripture passage: Ask Jesus a few very human questions, then grow quiet and listen. Then ask a few more, and listen again.

For example, Jesus, how long have you had this Kingdom-idea? When and where did you first get it? Did you talk it over with Mary? Did you ever try to reach John the Baptist with it?

Why in the world did you pick the Isaiah passage? Was that a favorite passage as a boy? Did you foresee the violent reaction it would bring? If so, how did you handle the tension you must have felt? Did you rehearse the reading with someone? Or consider but reject some other texts?

—Adapted from "A Method of Praying the Gospels" *by Francis Buck, S.J.*

MEDITATION

5

JESUS AT WORK

Spend another day reading St. Luke and becoming fascinated with Jesus, and at the many ways in which Jesus unifies His time and energy under one passion: "Inaugurate the Kingdom."

MEDITATIONS

a) *Disciples Pluck Grain*. Read Luke 6:1-5. Notice that the Disciples shouldn't have picked grain, according to the Law. But once they did, Jesus uses the occasion to make the point: "I am replacing the Law; I am beginning a New Order of things." He uses just every occasion.

> Lord, how we need a New Order Right Now! What a world if everyone were working together for your New Order! Even if just all Christians were. (Why aren't they?)

b) *The Man with the Withered Hand*. Read Luke 6:6-11. This is another miracle to keep getting Him attention, and to increase credibility for Jesus' Constant Message—to be proclaimed in season and out . . . .

> Lord, lest I wither because of . . . help me!

> Share your power with me so I can heal . . . or be healed.

Jesus, you fascinate me. And Jesus, do fascinate me.

Singlemindedness is good . . . but . . . how far do you
go, and I don't want to get fanatic. So, Lord . . . ?

c) *The Choice of the Twelve.* Read Luke 6:12-16. The number of Disciples is enlarged again in view of the Gigantic Work ahead.

Lord, have you some part for me in this gigantic
work?

Conclusion: Your reaction to the passages, or to something outstanding about them. Or to Jesus.

PRAYER HELPERS

If you are having trouble reacting personally, try to let your reaction be very, very simple, heart-felt, gut-level: What are you telling *me* in this incident, Lord? Or why do you talk this way?

Or ask Jesus some questions, as suggested in the Prayer Helps for the last meditation. Did you call some persons to be Apostles who said "No?" Then how did you feel? What sort of persons were you looking for, or was it variety you preferred? Did the way they looked or talked influence your choice? Had you had your eye on them for a while? And is growing toward intimacy with you going to bring me a relationship anything like the one you had with your Apostles, even though I remain in the priesthood of the people, rather than in priestly or religious life?

Or watch for the person in the scene with whom you can

identify. What might she or he be feeling? Or thinking or wondering?

Or—good question—does this event fire love for Jesus, or enthusiasm for his dream?

Or how does this passage apply to *people*, those near to you or those far?

MEDITATION

6

WALKING WITH JESUS

There is so much to be learned from these chapters! Please take one last meditation with Luke. Read Chapter 7 (and 8 if you like) with this commentary. This time try to reflect after each section, if moved. Notice how Jesus still seems so single-minded; so what does that mean?

MEDITATIONS

a) *The Centurion's Servant. The Widow's Son.* Luke 7:1-17. The Kingdom-connection is: more miracles are saying that God's healing power is now breaking *more* fully into history. Notice the need for faith, and how this miracle exceeds all the former in bringing even the dead to life.

> Lord, bring the best of *me* to life. Some of it is asleep.

> Lord, how much of goodness in other people, and all about the world, needs awakening.

> "Lord, I believe, help my unbelief"—a fine tolerance for ambivalence.

b) *The Stubborn Children.* Luke 7:31-34. Jesus is disappointed that all He is saying and doing isn't catching on fast enough.

101

I know, Lord, I am not catching on all that fast
either.

I suppose I am a little slow because of . . . my Ever
Present Obstacles, Lord. Mercy!

c) *The Women Who Served*. Luke 8:1-3. Jesus begins a move towards
equality for women's place in the Kingdom, though their place in society was
not acknowledged by the culture of the times.

Are not everyone's intuitive, sensitive and loving
qualities so needed in a world that is often insensitive?

Conclusion: How does Jesus impress you now? Could you be influencing
other people towards Jesus' dream? Or somehow be more deeply human,
more loving, or whatever? Maybe if others could see you as helpful, cheerful,
hopeful because you love Jesus . . . they too might be attracted . . . though
of course one doesn't want to parade piety . . . .

SEEDS OF ENCOURAGEMENT
FOR OUR KINGDOM EFFORTS

It is well to recall that absolutely everything we do for the Lord
will somehow have its good effect in the next life as well as in
this. Work for the Kingdom will surely be work we are
everlastingly proud of. And that applies to the most ordinary
work done in the spirit of "Thy Kingdom come, Thy will be
done."

By doing all the good we can in this life, we will rejoice in
Jesus' closer friendship forever, closer than had we lived more
selfishly. And we will also forever enjoy the thankful friendship
of people whom we have helped as we journeyed.

I consider the sufferings
of the present to be as nothing
compared with the glory
to be revealed in us.
Indeed the whole created world
eagerly awaits the revelation
of the children of God . . . .
because the world itself
will be freed from its slavery
to corruption
and share in the glorious freedom
of the children of God.
　　　　—*Romans 8*

(In Scripture Heaven is like...) "... the joy of my Father,
going home after separation from parents, a party, a
holiday, a wedding-day celebration, a happy ending, the
end of a long journey, a spring day after winter, the sun
rising after we have endured a long, sleepless night, the
finding of something precious we had lost, the arrival of a
longed-for letter, the end of an ordeal, rest and triumph
after winning a race or doing well, happiness after tears,
being found after being lost, hardess
after tears, being found after being lost, hard work
over, and time now to play."
　　　　—*Gerald O'Mahony, S.J.*

MEDITATION

7

THE KINGDOM TODAY

To help us become realistic, this meditation is about the present State of God's Earth, vis-a-vis Kingdom. So much good has been done and is being done by followers of Jesus. Heroes, saints, and ordinary people have built churches and hospitals. They have cared for the elderly, the sick and the poor, they have nourished family love, affection, and fidelity to duty—to name a few, though it is an endless list. At the same time, there is still so much to do, and so much harm is coming from apathy or forces of evil.

Beginning simply with the matter of food and hunger:

> Imagine ten children, at a table dividing up the food. The three healthiest load their plates with large portions, including most of the meat, fish, milk, and eggs. They eat what they want and discard the leftovers. Two other children get just enough to meet their basic requirements. The remaining five are left wanting. Three of them—sickly, nervous, apathetic children—manage to stave off the feeling of hunger by filling up on bread and rice. The other two cannot do even that. One dies of dysentery and the second from pneumonia which they are too weak to ward off.

> These children represent the human family. If present world food production were evenly divided among all the world's people, with a minimum of waste,

everyone would have enough. Barely enough, perhaps,
but enough.
—*Arthur Simon*, Bread for the World

In addition, as Jesus looks about the world, what does He see in the way of
organized crime, unjust profit taking, threats of war, human rights ignored—
even to torture and cruelty? Along with all the goodness, yes, what does He
see of broken faith and dishonesty; and where there is a capacity for
greatness, does He not see time and talents wasted?

Even in the ordinary personal relations of everyday living, it seems there is
still:

so much of hurt and loneliness, but
no oversupply of warmth and affection;
so much of ignoring others or putting them down,
but not enough support or affirmation
so much of intolerance and arguing, even anger and violence,
but not enough trying to understand or trying to be patient.

MEDITATION

Read John 3:16-17* and ask:

"Jesus, after all your efforts and ours, and after 2000 years, where are we? As
you look over the whole scene, what are you thinking, feeling, desiring?"

Or, if you prefer, consider how much good Jesus and His followers have
accomplished, how much is yet to be done, and what might be practical ways
right now to further The Work.

> *(John)
> *God so loved the world that He . . . gave His only
> Son . . . that the world might be saved through Him.*

Review the meditation and ask: Do I somehow—deep down—somehow want to be alongside Jesus in His great work for the Kingdom? If I can say Yes, this has been an especially significant meditation.

When it comes to influence, most of us have more than we think. Could you take measures to increase this talent? Is there any way you might consider using it more in connection with Jesus and His Work?

A possibility: Start something today for a better or happier world at home/work/school or recreation. After all, Jesus means business. Maybe start with just one person by trying to take a more positive attitude to them. Or maybe bring someone a bit of hope, or affirmation. Or run for office!

"Lord, some of us seem to have it so good in this world, while others, especially in the Third and Fourth Worlds, seem to have it so rotten. I don't understand that. Is there something I can do to shorten the gap?"

"Jesus,
I appreciate your dream
about the Kingdom.
But just to be working for your dream
Isn't enough.
I want your friendship too!"

The Kingdom was Jesus' Great Preoccupation. "So Jesus, please help me make it as real as possible for myself, too. I'm just not used to thinking about life that way every day."

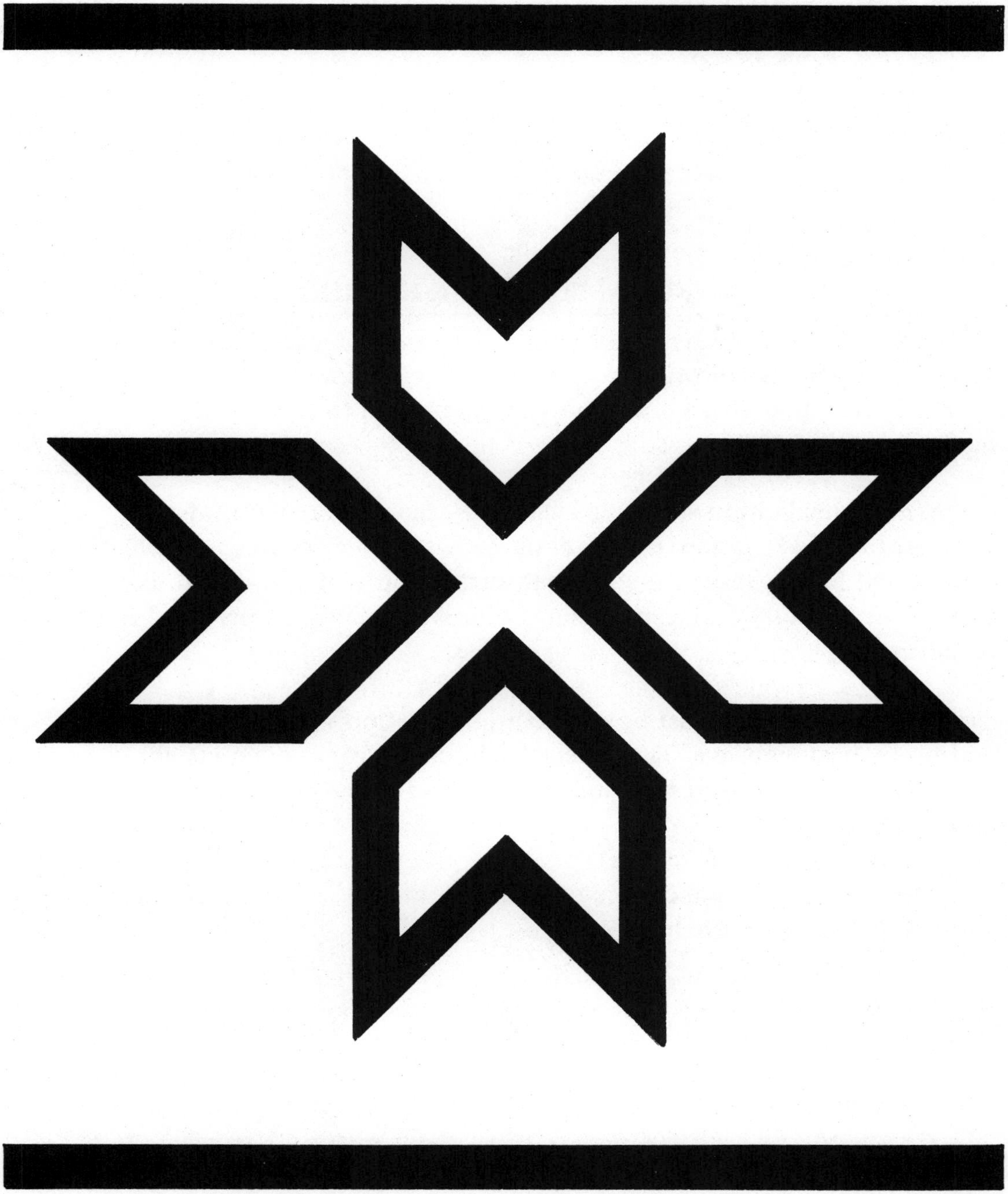

MEDITATION

8

PERSONALIZING THE KINGDOM

Following the lead of such masters in prayer as St. Ignatius and St. Teresa, spiritual writers and directors recommend making a meditation a second time over materials that strike you. This is a meditation to try the value of this method for yourself.

Choose any meditation where you felt you needed more time, or felt consolation or desolation. Consolation means feelings of peace, inclinations to love and follow Jesus, insights that attract you that you would like to linger over. Desolation means feelings of anxiety, unrest, resistance, worry, or burden.

Try to deepen the long-lasting effect this meditation will have on yourself and on the way you live. That effect might come from added insight or thinking, or simply from enjoying resting in a former insight with appreciation.

This could also be a fine chance to think about how you synchronize your work or family life with Jesus' vision.

MEDITATION

Your choice!

Or linger over a preceding meditation that brought consolation or desolation, that seemed more challenging or helpful, or that invited more time than you had available the first time.

SEEDS

If you were to present a highly creative version of your meditation with photographs, visuals, music, drama, or dance, how might you present it?

Can you think of Scripture passages or poetry to reflect the content of the meditation or your reactions to it?

In the meditations about the Kingdom—do you see Jesus and His values as signs of contradiction to many elements of our culture?

Jesus brought us "Kingdom" so we could enjoy hope, meaning in life, freedom, and gladness. It would be unfortunate if we were unmoved, or started feeling burdened or guilty because we cannot live His ideals fully. (See "Some Notes about Meditations 1-3" after Meditation 3 in this chapter.)

For long-term thinking, profound thinking, and much-needed reflection: consider what the Kingdom has to do with government, with family life, the Church, education, or/and communication media. As to when it is best to ponder such matters, let the Spirit lead.

MEDITATION

9

CARING FOR OTHERS

To be a Kingdom-person is to be a lover of people, all kinds of people—white, black, young, old, sick, rich, poor, nice, and not-so-nice, more or less beautiful, already born or still "on the way," up-and-in, or down-and-out, severely handicapped or just average—every person everywhere. God loves everybody.

Sometimes we could wish religion was only about loving Jesus in Heaven. Life would be easier. Or couldn't we love Him just in our hearts, in the Eucharist, or maybe in a few "nice" people? But to love people just as they are—why does He have to identify with *everyone*?

MEDITATION

"Jesus, I should *so* like to find You in everyone I meet. With sensitivity, care, open to each person's beauty, uniqueness and pain. So . . . I ask:

"Jesus, how do you see yourself in people? How would you like me to see you?" Read Luke 10:23-37* and pray as you feel moved.

> *(Luke)
> *"Which of these three, in your opinion, was neighbor*
> *to the man who fell in with the robbers?"*
> *"The one who treated him with compassion."*
> *Jesus said to him, "Then go and do the same."*

Some time I am going to have to think whether this is primarily what I want to do with my life: Be Jesus to others. And if that is my primary aim, then how do earning a livelihood, caring for my family, etc., fit in? I have a lot to pray about! (Being Jesus: Doing all the good you can, lovingly.)

Who can I let be Jesus *to me*? Some people will never let anyone do anything for them. This is a mistake. How can others be Jesus, if no one will accept?

The Temptation of Active Christians is to become Functional Christians; that is, to concentrate on getting the work done, lots of work, to the neglect of staying a "people person." They can become too busy for love, people, or caring; and too tired for affection or prayer. Would you agree or disagree? Finding time for prayer can be a problem. So can finding time for people. Where does all the time go?

MEDITATION

10

WHERE AM I GOING?

This is a day just to sit for a while in front of Jesus in the Blessed Sacrament; or by myself in a quiet room, or with favorite music; or in an outdoor scene of some beauty, just so I can be in quiet and listen for the movement of the Spirit.

MEDITATION

Read Mark 6:30-32*.
Because of these thirty meditations, how am I different? What has God been saying, or what has Jesus? Are changes called for in my approach to prayer, people, Himself? Could the meditations be speaking to my hopes and dreams, my anxieties or burdens?

And there are many more: they could be speaking to what I want from life, or what life is asking of me. They could be talking to my love for Jesus or the Father, to my basic motives, my sense of values, priorities. . . . anything.

"From this series of meditations, what are you saying, Lord? Please speak, I would like to listen."

> *(Mark)
> *The Apostles returned to Jesus and reported to him*

all that they had done and what they had taught. He said to them, "Come by yourselves to an out-of-the-way place and rest a little."

SEEDS

Why not take a few days off from meditating? Yes, really. A rest, even from good things occasionally, can help spiritual growth.

Consider too the possibility of a retreat, taking time away from work and family to be with the Lord at a Retreat House, or just by yourself.

LOVE

I love you
Not only for what you are,
But for what I am
When I am with you.

I love you
Not only for what
You have made of yourself,
But for what
You are making of me.

I love you
For the part of me
That you bring out;
I love you

For putting your hand
Into my heaped-up heart
And passing over
All the foolish, weak things
that you can't help
Dimly seeing there.
And for drawing out
Into the light
All the beautiful belongings
That no one else had looked
Quite far enough to find.

I love you because you
Are helping me to make
Of the lumber of my life
Not a tavern
But a temple;
Out of the works
Of my every day
Not a reproach
But a song. . . .
　　　　—*Author Unknown*

So, Lord—where do we go from here?

REVIEW OF AIDS TO PRAYER

If you are having any difficulty meditating, dryness, can't concentrate, etc., check on the following:

> Physically indisposed, nervous, or tense.
> Emotional upset, anxiety, deeply hurt feelings.
>   (A worry about health, children or love?)
> Dry period—one of those ups and downs that
>   go with anything in life. (At times we
>   must wait on the Lord.)
> Lack of proper place or atmosphere of quiet.
> Lack of unwinding, or proper preparation, or
>   of becoming recollected in the presence of
>   God.
> Need for more time, or more motivation and
>   appreciation for prayer. For some, more
>   reverent posture.
> Lack of method.
> Doubts about faith.
> Can't feel right with God because of disorderly
>   attachment to sin, object, person,
>   ambition. . . .
> Feeling overburdened by high ideals, by trying
>   too hard, or being discouraged at lack of
>   progress.
> Not listening enough in your prayer.
> God's call to leave thought and conversation-
>   type prayer, and to react simply with an
>   emotion or affection.

Try to recall what turned you on in prayer and incorporate *that*—whatever it was—into your prayer.

Possibly it would be better for YOU to start with the Jesus Prayer, or Centering Prayer, or some form of Eastern Prayer for an ordinary meditation; and you could use *these* meditations for spiritual reading each day.

Something important for prayer: a disposition, an inner desire for God. Put another way, I am made for God. And I ache after Him. With some it's connatural. In others He'll stir it if asked. Go on the assumption that Love, that delicious, bittersweet attraction, is for you!

If after checking on all the above, difficulty still persists, Do Something. Re-read the prayer directions in Chapters 1, 2, and 3. Talk with the Lord; then with a friend, physician, counselor, or spiritual guide, as appropriate.

When to pray. It's best to find time when nothing else is going on. If you can't, you can first read the meditation thoughtfully and finish it while bathing, driving, bicycling, jogging, doing housework or chores that do not demand full and continuous attention.

In what posture? Spiritual writers are nearly unanimous: In whatever posture helps you pray. Sitting, standing, lying (you may fall asleep), walking about, whatever. They also agree that a certain reverence to the posture frequently helps too, sitting somewhat straight, not too relaxed, etc. The mild physical tonus lifts spirit as well as body!

EXPANDING PRAYER HORIZONS

The meditations in the chapters of this book are only beginnings, mere suggestions as to topics for prayer. The following are a few samples of other ways in which each chapter could be extended.

For Chapter One, "Removing Obstacles and Sensing His Love," you could create meditations such as:

A litany of thankgiving for everything in sight.

An eye-opening search for God's presence in objects; or in persons; or in events during any one hour of your day.

You could talk with Jesus about what prevents groups or even nations from sensing His love—or leaders of nations; and all the consequences that follow. You could then pray for their healing.

Poetry, literature, lyrics to popular songs, TV presentations, newspapers and magazines could all be turned to prayer. Many popular songs can be sung of divine love as well as of human love.

As to "Communicating Over Everything," Chapter Two, you might share with Jesus your day at the office, in the fields, at home, at school, in the shop. Such communication would make a fine evening prayer.

You might share feelings with the Lord about people in your life, beginning with your family, conversing about and pausing to pray for each. Then you could pray about other people, the pleasant and the irritating, and finally about the Family of Humankind, or about the state of family life in our nation.

As to the Kingdom Meditations in Chapter Three, these could *really* enlarge your way of praying. They could enlarge your vision far beyond the Jesus-and-I spirituality, which is both needful for and inadequate to full Christian spirituality.

You might consider in some detail what Jesus' dream of Kingdom could mean for some one area of business or the economy, of politics or human rights, or one of the questions about arms, hunger, or the integration of races. You could keep gathering information in the area and praying over it as you do. If such topics have overtones close to your local church or community, those situations could furnish starting points for prayer.

To the reader:

I hope you have enjoyed *Intimacy With Jesus*.
Its composition has been a labor of love
and each day I pray for those who use it.
Please pray for me that I may have the opportunity
to follow this book with two others:
one on Jesus' Public Life, and the second
on His Passion, Death, and Resurrection.

Peace, such as only He can give.
　　　—*Richard J. Huelsman, S.J.*